PRAISE FOR *REFLECTIONS OF IMMANUEL*

"Advent is the season of the church year in which we wait. We
wait for the celebration of Christ's birth in history, we wait
for Christ's return, and we wait for Christ to come to us right
where we are, especially in the midst of the cold and the dark
of the winter seasons of our lives. *Reflections of Immanuel* is
a book for all those who wait. Ranging across the whole of
Scripture from Genesis to Revelation, Scott Lencke invites us
to imaginatively enter story after story—from Abraham to
Ahaz, from Job to John—in order to remind us that no matter
how long and cold the winter, no matter how dark the night,
we are not alone. The One for whom we wait is already in our
midst: Immanuel. God is with us."

—K. C. IRETON, AUTHOR OF *THE CIRCLE OF SEASONS:
MEETING GOD IN THE CHURCH YEAR*

"In the midst of the cacophony of Christmas consumerist
voices, Scott Lencke helps us to take a step back, breathe,
and listen to the deep meaning of Advent and Christmas.
With insight and wit he shows how the well-known stories
of the birth of Jesus are rooted in the stories and prophecies
of the Hebrew Scriptures, in ways we might have forgotten
or never learned."

—ARMAND LÉON VAN OMMEN, LECTURER IN PRACTICAL
THEOLOGY, UNIVERSITY OF ABERDEEN

"'Getting ready for Christmas' is commonly experienced as an uptick in the speed and frenzy of life. We rush, scurry, and get caught up in the 'mall religion' around us. With grace and insight, Scott Lencke offers us a well-trodden but forgotten alternative path—the Advent way. Leading us to contemplate markers left by prophets, psalmists, sages, and evangelists along the road, Scott accompanies us on a slow, conversational walk to the manger of Immanuel."

—MIKE MERCER, AUTHOR OF *WALKING HOME TOGETHER: SPIRITUAL GUIDANCE AND PRACTICAL ADVICE FOR THE END OF LIFE*

"Entering Advent means entering darkness. Not everyone can handle this darkness. Fewer still can sit in it, steep in it, and learn from it. *Reflections of Immanuel* invites us to dwell in the darkness. With wisdom drawn from pop culture, master storytellers, and theologians, *Reflections of Immanuel* looks beyond the luminescence of Christmas and invites us to dwell in the dusky world of lament, grief, and the God who promises to come near."

—TOM FUERST, SACRED CONVERSATIONALIST, BLUFF CITY CHURCH, MEMPHIS, TENNESSEE

Reflections of Immanuel

Reflections of Immanuel

SCOTT LENCKE

WIPF & STOCK · Eugene, Oregon

REFLECTIONS OF IMMANUEL

Wipf & Stock
An Imprint of Wipf and Stock Publishers
199 W. 8th Ave., Suite 3
Eugene, OR 97401

www.wipfandstock.com

PAPERBACK ISBN: 978-1-5326-1833-8
HARDCOVER ISBN: 978-1-4982-4382-7
EBOOK ISBN: 978-1-4982-4381-0

Manufactured in the U.S.A.   08/28/20

Cat, Caleb, Joshua, and Mattheus.

God starts out where we start out: a child is born. He submerges himself in our biology, our psychology, our history. He becomes one of us so we can become what he is. He doesn't terrorize us with doomsday signs. He doesn't crush us with superior knowledge. He doesn't tease us with mysterious clues. He is here with us, in Jesus. God's way of revealing himself to us and giving himself to us is Jesus.

—Eugene Peterson[1]

1. Peterson, *As Kingfishers Catch Fire*, 139.

Contents

Acknowledgments

Brent Diggs and Harold Toboggans.
Crosstown Concourse and French Truck Coffee, Memphis.
Renewal Church and the Puritan Reading Group.
Father, Son, and Spirit.

INTRODUCTION

Christmas Can Wait

The church is not fighting against time. The Christian does
not, or at any rate need not, consider time an enemy. Time is
not doing him any harm, time is not standing between him
and anything he desires. Time is not robbing him of anything
he treasures.

–THOMAS MERTON[1]

Each year we cycle back around to an all-important date: December
25th. It's a day remembered and celebrated around the world, both
in the church and society at large.[2] In American culture, this date
is bookended by Thanksgiving (along with the infamous Black Friday) and New Year's Day. A five-to-six-week festive holiday period
within American life.

In actuality, if we step back a bit more, peering into the different stores and retail outlets across our land, we see November 1st
is now reserved as the more attractive marker to start the holiday
season. As the calendar page turns from October to November, the
black and orange of Halloween decorations are removed from the
shelves and replaced with shades of red and green, Christmas trees,
stringed lights, and a host of other seasonal selections.

1. Merton, *Seasons of Celebration*, 37.

2. The Eastern Church actually celebrates Christmas on January 6th, which
is the Feast of Epiphany.

1

With the arrival of November 1st, we are now offered a full two-month window into all things Christmas. At least according to the American storyline.

I have never been shy about my love for Christmas. It has always been a magical time, filled with beauty and inspiration. I was known to sound forth the Christmas tunes early, even as we stepped out of October and into November. I once pondered if it was appropriate to start listening to holiday tunes on October 25th, since it gave an exact two-month lead up to Christmas Day.

I was that guy. I went all out, at times, to the annoyance of my wife.

So, yes, the lead up to Christmas has always been my favorite. The sights, the sounds, and the smells—all of it. I also appreciate a time of leaves gently falling to the ground and temperatures slowly dipping toward freezing (unfortunately, I'm in the American South where it seldom drops below freezing).

While many of these details speak of a unique experience within the "holiday season," I have gradually come to realize how much of it may have pulled us away from many more important things. We may have become enamored with the insatiable desire for more rather than live in a place of contentment with what we already have. Instead of faithfully stewarding a grander narrative that God's people have been telling for two thousand years, the consumerist storyline may have diverted our attention. K.C. Ireton states it this way:

> Unfortunately, Advent as a liturgical season focused on waiting and inward preparation has disappeared culturally; even in the church, we often ignore its call to reflection. Advent has become "the holiday season," and we measure it in the number of shopping days left before the twenty-fifth of December rolls around. We cram the weeks before Christmas with parties and shopping and decorating and the wrapping of gifts and the mailing of cards inscribed with words like "Peace on earth" or "Joy to the world," even though we too often feel anything but

peaceful and joyful as we scurry around checking things off our endless to-do list.[3]

Ireton describes my own life—and the battle is still very present today.

It's as if we have walked through the wardrobe in *The Chronicles of Narnia*, and we have responded as Edmund did upon meeting the White Witch. Just as he could not get enough of the Witch's delicious Turkish delight, we seem unable to halt the pull toward more and more stuff. And we don't even know how all this stuff came to be. We just know we want it—the twinkles, trinkets, and toys—as much as we can get. We are mesmerized like an insect drawn to the purple-tinted light of a bug zapper. The hustle and bustle seem to never end, even after making promises that next year will be different.

It's no surprise that the church in modern America has embraced the spiritual practice of consumerism itself. The desire for more and more is spiritual, in that it calls to our *whole* selves—heart, mind, and body. James K.A. Smith refers to this cultural reality as the *mall religion*. He offers, "Indeed, the genius of mall religion is that actually it operates with a more holistic, affective, embodied anthropology (or theory of the human person) than the Christian church tends to assume!" What he's saying is that this "mall religion" speaks to our entire being. Smith continues: "Because our hearts are oriented primarily by desire, by what we love, and because those desires are shaped and molded by the habit-forming practices in which we participate, it is the rituals and practices of the mall—the liturgies of mall and market—that shape our imaginations and how we orient ourselves to the world."[4]

The sights, sounds, smells, and tastes—those rituals and practices—of all kinds of shopping centers beckon us. The invitation isn't merely for those who seek out stores or surf the web during Black Friday. This religion is all-pervasive, finding its way into our homes and workplaces, our television streaming services and media outlets, every nook and cranny it possibly can. And it's also

3. Ireton, *The Circle of Seasons*, 21.
4. Smith, *Desiring the Kingdom*, 24.

found its way into our churches and spirituality. Walter Bruegge-mann observes how the church (or the "prophetic community," as he calls us) and its worship have been "replaced by television jingles that find us singing consumerism ideology to ourselves and to each other."[5] It is truly everywhere.

Service after service.

Performance after performance.

Jingle after jingle.

Production after production.

Hour after hour.

American Christianity has become predominantly product-based (supplying those who already have much) rather than ser-vant-based (emptying ourselves on behalf of others who have little). While this consumerist spirituality has infected much of Western Christianity, we Americans lead the way!

This approach is perhaps one reason why Christmas (along with Easter) is the most tiresome period for church leaders and staff. We can hardly sustain the efforts that the mall religion asks of us. Yet because we sing the carols of the season and place a nativity scene somewhere on our stage, it perhaps allows for us to stamp out the gentle whisper inside that just might prompt us to consider something better, more enchanting.

Don't get me wrong. As I said, I, too, enjoy many of our holi-day delights. I do. But over the years, my attention has been drawn toward something else.

It's a story.

Even more, it's the *tangible* telling of a story.

Not just *that* story, the one we read about at the beginning of the Gospels of Matthew and Luke. But I also speak of a story that's been unfolding since the Gospel writers penned their accounts long ago. The one the church has been telling for centuries, the ancient path she's been walking for some time now.

We all love stories, right?

We all love to turn the pages or watch film frames flash before our eyes, to encounter our favorite characters, hear the dialogue,

5. Brueggemann, *The Prophetic Imagination*, 17.

and be stirred by the soundtrack. Stories of all kinds draw us in like very little else.

The church has been telling a story now for two thousand years. We find it within the church's liturgical calendar. It starts with the most unique story—the announcement and birth of Immanuel, "God with us."

However, perhaps this story has been flattened, replaced by the many things available at the click of a button. Is it possible that in our overcommitment to the cultural sights, sounds, and smells of the season, we have lost a sense of the beauty of the more captivating story? Is it possible all the "stuff" has tempered our collective remembrance of God's story? Maybe we are under a spell as Edmund was.

It's not just the message, but also how we communicate that message. Would the depth of the message serve as mere fodder for a daytime talk show? Do we hold the media and music teams to a seasonal production worthy of a Hollywood film? Are we looking to the preacher to wow us with humor and intellect comparable to one of the great TED Talks? While we may find some truth present within each of these, our methods have diverted our attention to something less meaningful.

Now don't go throwing out your trees, unplugging your lights, or throwing away the presents. Don't oust your new Advent preaching series just yet (unless it's entitled, "Manger Things": a play off the hit show *Stranger Things*).

Then again, perhaps that's just what you need to do. I'll leave that in your capable hands. But I would offer we most definitely need to employ tactics that will help us shed our shopping-center religion.

Where might we begin? How might we initiate the detachment process?

By waiting.

The subversive yet radical act of waiting.

This means we consider that Christmas can wait.

If we are able to avoid the prevailing pull of American religion and consider how to walk the ancient path the church has taken, then Christmas can wait.

Part of our commercialized culture includes gratifying our-selves whenever we desire—from food to Netflix to shopping to social media to sex. To practice waiting, even a little bit, is an essential practice. It's just that we don't believe in waiting—nor abstaining—any longer. It's too old-fashioned. But we wait for other things. Why not Christmas?

Christmas can wait.

We wait for autumn or spring to roll in gradually.

Christmas can wait.

We wait for the sun to peek its head over the horizon.

Christmas can wait.

We wait in line for our lattes and cold brews.

Christmas can wait.

We can practice waiting.

In a season of pause, we learn the practice of not bowing to the culturally formed golden calf. We can do this because we first need to journey through the season of Advent before we come to Christmas.

I hope this little book reminds us and refocuses us on what the church has celebrated for two millennia. It asks us to celebrate Christmas. We will get to that. However, it first invites us to join the Advent path. The secular calendar restarts on January 1st, but the church year begins on the first day of the Advent season. This makes Advent the entrypoint into the wider Christian story.

You may not even be aware of the church calendar. It may sound old-fashioned. I was there not too long ago. Or, perhaps, some of you walk its rhythmic patterns with great attention. As Robert Webber reminds us, "The church has been entrusted with the meaning of all time. The world does not know the meaning of its own history, but the church does. Through the discipline of the Christian year, the church proclaims the meaning of time and of the history of the world." We are to know and tell the meaning of time. As he later puts it, "[T]he church year is the Word proclaimed and enacted."[6]

6. Webber, *Ancient-Future Time*, 26–28.

The church calendar is not an irrelevant tradition given to lull us to sleep or, worse, lead us to our spiritual graves with dead religion. Rather, the church year, including Advent, has been given to us as part of the story to assist in forming hearts, minds, and bodies. Jeremiah speaks of the *ancient paths* and the *good way* (Jer 6:16). The church calendar is, I believe, just that.

My hope is that these "reflections of Immanuel" will offer something authentic about what God has done, is doing, and will do in Christ. Moreover, I desire for the church's grand story to indeed draw us in. That grand story opens with its own chapter 1, entitled Advent, beginning four Sundays before Christmas and running through Christmas Eve. The word *advent* simply means "arrival" or "coming." For Christians, it's a word that speaks to the arrival of Christ into the world. But it also points to his second advent, the one where he arrives to complete all he started long ago. There will be a renewal of all things, a making of all things right and good as God desires.

I want to celebrate Christmas. Very much so! But I also want to wait and walk through the season of Advent. I desire to guard against a heightened sense of distraction found in too many elements of American culture. I want to walk with God's people, the church now and the church historic. I want to do so in reflection, contemplation, anticipation, and hope.

I want to wait for Christmas.

I want to wait for the most tangible reminder that God is with us, Immanuel.

I invite you to wait for Christmas.

INTRODUCTION: CHRISTMAS CAN WAIT

Questions for Reflection

1. Does your church community celebrate the season of Advent? If so, what particular elements stand out that make this season special? If not, how do you believe your church could celebrate this season in the future?

2. Do you believe that consumerism—the desire to have more and more stuff—has taken over our focus during the Advent and Christmas seasons? If so, what things can we set in place, both personally and collectively, to help Christians guard against bowing to this idol of "more-ism"?

How the Theologian Stole Christmas

The Grinch *hated* Christmas! The whole Christmas season!
Now, please don't ask why. No one quite knows the reason.
It *could* be his head wasn't screwed on just right.
It *could* be perhaps his shoes were too tight.
But I think that the most likely reason of all
May have been that his heart was two sizes too small.

−DR. SEUSS[1]

It was Christmas morning. Jimmy was just coming around from a restful sleep. He scanned the room with squinted, sleepy eyes, and then glanced at the clock on the nightstand just next to his bed.

It was just past seven in the morning.

Jimmy bolted out of bed, grabbed his Santa hat (to match his Santa pajamas), flung his bedroom door open, and headed for the stairs. He conquered them two by two as an effort to get to the living room as quickly as possible.

He had one thing on his mind: Christmas gifts.

Jimmy hunkered to his knees, checking the tags on the gifts.

His eyes widened. *This one's for me!* he thought to himself.

Oh, that one is for dad. Another for me. Mom, mom, me, dad.

---

1. Seuss, *How the Grinch Stole Christmas,* 7–12, emphasis his.

After browsing the presents, Jimmy's eyes moved to the hand-knit stockings hung above the ash-laced fireplace. His grandmother had sewn the seasonal images on them herself.

Jimmy's hands cupped the bottom of his stocking. It, too, was filled with goodies.

Just then, he heard the sound of creaking planks as feet gently strode across the hardwood floors. Expecting to see either his mom or dad, Jimmy stumbled backward in shock at what he saw. A strange figure stood before him. Unkempt beard and hair, brown corduroy coat with elbow patches, a button-up dress shirt with tie, pleated trousers, and scuffed-up Hush Puppies?

Jimmy had never seen this man before and wondered how he got into the house.

"Whoooo are yooou?" Jimmy stuttered with parched mouth and racing heart.

"Why, I am the Theologian of Christmas Past!" the man remarked boisterously in a striking British accent.

"The what?" Jimmy asked with a furrowed brow.

"Son, why, I am here to inform you about the indelible truth of Christmas. I've arrived to remind you of the babe's story from long ago, but not just the story of his birth. I have come to *show* you a story about how people have remembered that birth throughout time."

"To *show* me?" replied Jimmy.

"Why, yes. One cannot simply listen to this story. We have got to go on a journey to encounter the story, one of centuries past."

"You mean we're going somewhere?"

"Of course. As one who's been granted the power to travel into the past, each year I arrive at someone's home to take them back in time to reveal the true meaning of Christmas. More than the gifts. More than the lights. More than Frosty and Rudolph. Now come, we must be going."

"B-b-b-but, I don't know you," Jimmy stuttered. "I'm okay staying right here to celebrate Christmas with my family."

"Son, trust me. I am only here to assist. Take my hand."

The young boy cautiously arose and shuffled over to the front door. There he grabbed his overcoat, knit scarf, and gloves. He then slowly scooted over to the unknown man and hesitantly grabbed his right hand. At that very moment, the window flew up. Jimmy could feel the cold draft of the winter's morning air.

Just then, both he and the man began to lift off the ground slowly.

"Hold on!" the man called out.

Jimmy held on as tight as he could, for it felt like they were being sucked out of the window into the open air.

At that moment, Jimmy jerked out of his sleep and sat up in bed. He reached over to grab the glass of water on the nightstand, taking a sip to satisfy his parched throat. He peeked at the clock. It read the same time as when he previously looked at it.

Jimmy slowly came to it, breathing in and out of his nose at a calming pace. His heart rate was soaring. He closed his eyes and continued the slow breathing.

His mind went back to the dream.

It had to have been a dream. He was back in bed. Nothing he'd just experienced happened, right?

Where did that dream come from? It seemed so real, Jimmy thought to himself.

He rolled out of bed, then quietly opened the bedroom door. Gradually descending the stairs, he made his way down to the living room. As he neared the bottom, Jimmy stopped and peered around the room. Everything seemed normal. The tree stood alit, presents were under the tree, and stockings still hung on the mantle.

All of a sudden, Jimmy felt a cold gust of air move by him. The hairs on his neck and arms stood up. He pivoted to check the window, the one through which he and the man had exited.

It was open!

Perhaps it wasn't merely a dream.

Perhaps he had been visited by the Theologian of Christmas Past.

How the Theologian Stole Christmas.

That's the title of this chapter. It could just have easily been *How the Preacher Stole Christmas.* The title is a play off the well-known

Dr. Seuss book, *How the Grinch Stole Christmas!*. Even if we haven't read the book, we've probably at least seen a film version.

As you may also be aware, the storyline is a spin-off of Charles Dickens's *A Christmas Carol*. Rather than the Ghost of Christmas Past visiting Ebenezer Scrooge, we find the Theologian of Christmas Past visiting Jimmy.

After writing the introductory chapter to this book, my insecurities came to the forefront. I wondered if my musings would suck the life out of something like the season of Christmas. I pondered if I was overanalyzing a cultural problem. That's what theologians do, right? They overthink the simple stuff. By the way, I do have a corduroy jacket with elbow patches, but I do not wear pleated pants.

Keep your theology to yourself!

Theology is helpful, but don't let it ruin life!

I recognize that a book that opens with a challenge to shed some of our cultural Christmas practices can come across as sucking the fun out of something so, well, fun.

Perhaps I'm merely imagining the objections in my head. Maybe I'm stepping into my own dream to match Jimmy's.

I am not against cultural aspects of the holiday season. But I do believe there is a better way: a way of beauty and life that Advent and the church calendar can kindle. As Robbie Castleman notes, "The central significance of marking the liturgical year is to help shape the Christocentric reality of the church. Jesus's story is the Christian story, the foundational story that shapes, tests, and vindicates Christian life and faith."[2]

While this concept may sound crusty and outdated for some, the reality is that we all—both in our church and personal setting— embrace liturgy. We all welcome a "rhythm of life" that shapes who we are. It's just that the church has too willingly allowed a very different rhythm to dictate its story. Of course, the church's liturgical rhythm is not meant to provide a corner in which we hide away from the world. Instead, it offers something tangibly beautiful to shape who we are in Christ and to call others to join in that story.

---

2. Castleman, *Story-Shaped Worship*, 36.

This is why I think it's worth waiting for Christmas and walking with the church during the season of Advent.

As Advent arrives and you dive into this little book of reflections, again, I hope that it will help shape us a little more into the renewed image of Christ. The ancients waited centuries for Christ's arrival—and we still find ourselves waiting centuries for his final arrival to make all things right. But I propose that we journey with many of our forefathers and mothers.

They walked it.

We walk it.

Those to come will one day walk it, too.

As the writer to the Hebrews reminds us, "These were all commended for their faith, yet none of them received what had been promised, since God had planned something better for us so that only *together with us* would they be made perfect" (Heb 11:39–40, emphasis mine).

As we wait for and walk the well-worn path, laying aside many of the mall religion's ways, perhaps we will be immersed in a better Advent story. We can then move into a celebratory Christmas, both on December 25th and for the full twelve days of the season.

Maybe this isn't *How the Theologian Stole Christmas*.

Perhaps it's all about *How the Church Recovered Christmas*.

I invite you, the reader, to wait for Christmas by joining the church's rhythmic story of Advent. As we patiently move through the season, and then into Christmas itself, this little book will hopefully offer fresh insights on familiar Scripture passages and themes. My prayer is that these brief reflections will stir our affections toward a more genuine love for Immanuel, God with us.

POST-INTRODUCTION: HOW THE
THEOLOGIAN STOLE CHRISTMAS

Questions for Reflection

1. In Jeremiah 6:16, the prophet calls the people to "ask for the ancient paths." Do you believe the church of today struggles to walk the ancient paths? If so, how might the modern-day church get past the barrier of being closed off to ancient practices?

2. We have considered how the church should perhaps look to walk a rhythm quite different from the one we find in our culture. What particular cultural rhythms do you think we should discard? Are there some spiritual rhythms that you believe your church could employ during the Advent season to help focus on what God has done in Jesus Christ?

CHAPTER 1

Advent Story as Ancient Story

*These are the words [Jesus] read, these were the stories he
knew, these were the songs he sang.*

−CHRIS WRIGHT[1]

When it comes to the church and her Advent messages, the usual
places to head are the Gospels of Matthew or Luke. The reason is
that both of these provide us with the birth and infant accounts of
Jesus. We get Joseph's angle in Matthew and Mary's outlook in Luke.

Opening Matthew, it may be that we find ourselves jumping
past the first seventeen verses. There are too many names, so it's on
to verse 18.

This is how the birth of Jesus the Messiah came about . . .

Not a bad place to start, right?

Well, perhaps not. That isn't the beginning of the Christmas
story. At least not from the viewpoint of the Gospel accounts. For
Matthew, a Jew writing to a Jewish community in the latter part of
the first century, the story begins with verse 1.

*This is the genealogy of Jesus the Messiah the son of David, the
son of Abraham.*

A Jewish disciple of Jesus is much more in touch with Jewish
storylines than we might be. The problem is that as we dive into

1. Wright, *Knowing Jesus*, ix.

those early verses of Matthew 1, we aren't too sure what to make of all those names. We can't even pronounce most of them.

It may be worth noting that Matthew's genealogy is relatively simplified compared to other listings in the Bible. For example, take a peek at the first nine chapters of First Chronicles. Ouch! Yes, nine whole chapters of names, tracking from Adam all the way down to the great-great-great-great-great-great-great-great-great-great-great-great-grandsons of King Saul (I may have missed a "great" in there).

Insert the sound of snoring.

But Matthew is telling a story. One that doesn't merely begin at verse 18. It kicks off with Jesus's family line primarily because it connects the story of the Messiah to the story of Israel in the Hebrew Scriptures.[2] Chris Wright reminds us: the stories of the Old Testament were the stories Jesus knew. They were the ones his parents would have told him at bedtime and the readings he would have heard each week in the Jewish synagogue.

The creation.
The flood.
The exodus.
The giving of the Torah.[3]
The crossing of the sea.
The conquering of the land.
The battles.
The judges.
The kings.
The songs.
The prophets.
The promises.
The visions.

2. Many like to refer to the Old Testament as the Hebrew Scriptures, since it was written by the Hebrew-Jewish people and stands as their specific set of holy writings. I am fine referring to this portion as either the Old Testament or the Hebrew Scriptures.

3. The Hebrew word *torah* means "instruction," and is usually translated as "law." When the word is capitalized, it refers to the specific Hebrew-Jewish Law as given through Moses.

Every story begins with "once upon a time," including Jesus's. He had stepped into an already-unfolding drama that God had been directing for centuries and centuries. And his story makes much more sense in light of the chapters that were written before his.

Even the names carry greater significance than is first apparent. Names point to mini-stories within the larger account. If I say the names Aragorn and Frodo, or Harry and Dumbledore, these mean something to modern-day people. They each convey tales that, perhaps, stir the emotions and the imagination. The same would have been true for Jews when they read these ancient names in the Bible.

Abraham, Isaac, and Jacob.

Boaz, Ruth, Jesse, and David.

Solomon, Jehoshaphat, Uzziah, and Hezekiah.

Name after name; story after story.

These names and their stories unmistakably connect to Jesus. He arrives on the scene because of these people and their lives.

The importance of the ancient accounts is seen in greater detail as Matthew goes on to quote many of the prophets at Jesus's birth and during his early childhood. The Immanuel promise of Isaiah and the Bethlehem prophecy in Micah directly connect to his story. He is the great deliverer of God's people, having been delivered himself from a tyrant's massacre of babies just as Moses had centuries prior. But these Bible references are not random quotes given to merely "prove" Jesus is God's Messiah. They embed him within the old Jewish story.

Jesus will again root himself in Israel's narrative following his resurrection from the grave. On the road to Emmaus, he reveals: "This is what I told you while I was still with you: Everything must be fulfilled that is written about me in the Law of Moses, the Prophets and the Psalms" (Luke 24:44).

The Law of Moses, the Prophets, and the Psalms.

These represented the three "sections" of the old Hebrew Bible. Jesus is announcing that his story is found right across the entire plot of the ancient Scriptures.

What might this mean for *us* as we arrive at the season of Advent?

For starters, there is beauty in noting that something much grander than we can imagine has been unfolding over time. Something bigger is at play here—more significant than you, me, our community, our church, our day, and our time.

It's like studying the planets, the stars, the galaxies, and the universe. Once we start, we must step back and realize not only what a little blip we are but also what a pin-prick even our own planet is in the midst of it all. It is mind-bogglingly awesome!

I don't know about you, but I find solace in the fact that my story is part of another more magnificent than my own, even beyond what I can fathom. I don't lose hope reading words like these: "What is your life? You are a mist that appears for a little while and then vanishes" (Jas 4:14).

Our story, though important, is surrounded by a great cloud of witnesses (Heb 12:1). I believe that is something worth reveling in.

Furthermore, considering our own time and place, we will do well to remember that God is active in our story. Right here, right now. It is good to recall and recount God's activity in our lives. This roots us in the tangible—the things we can touch, see, hear, taste, and smell. In this, we find resolve, reassurance, and hope—even while we, at times, still experience pain, loss, and grief as we walk out life.

God was at work in the lives of Abraham, Isaac, and Jacob. His grace is noted for Boaz, Ruth, Jesse, and David. His activity was clearly amongst Solomon, Jehoshaphat, Uzziah, and Hezekiah.

The same is true for each of us.

However, it not only means that God is active in our personal stories. It also means he's engaged in our *collective* stories. By the Spirit, God is shaping families, neighborhoods, local church communities, and the people groups of our world. Our lens may be largely individualistic, but the ancients viewed things much more communally. We see this most in God's promise to Abraham: "all peoples on earth will be blessed through you" (Gen 12:3). God's restoration work through the likes of Abraham and Christ was to impact all peoples. Those chosen by God—Abraham, Jesus, you, and I—are part of a group of people collectively called to bless others. How can we allow for God's work in our corporate story to propel us to love and serve the peoples of this world in their story?

Advent is a time that connects us to an ancient, collective story.

Immanuel shows up in Christ. Immanuel shows up where we are. Immanuel shows up in Christ's world. Immanuel shows up in our world.

Let's remember the Advent story. Let's tell the Advent story.

It's one worth telling well.

This is the genealogy [or story] of Jesus the Messiah . . .

CHAPTER 1: ADVENT STORY AS ANCIENT STORY

Questions for Reflection

1. Would you say the Old Testament story is more foreign than familiar to you? If so, what makes it so foreign? What are some practical steps you could take to help better know and understand the Old Testament?

2. Take a moment to read Matthew 1:1–17. Which names, along with their stories, are known to you? Now pick one that is not familiar to you and read that person's story in the Old Testament (if their story can be located). What insights come to you as you read about someone with whom you are unfamiliar?

CHAPTER 2

The Original Immanuel

God starts out where we start out: a child is born. He submerges himself in our biology, our psychology, our history. He
becomes one of us so we can become what he is.

–EUGENE PETERSON[1]

The year was approximately 735 BCE.[2] War was imminent. Nerves
were on edge. A few small, Middle Eastern nations found themselves in deep unrest as they considered their plight amongst the
world power of their day, Assyria.

The record that we read in Scripture tells us of a particular
king—Ahaz. Isaiah 7 recounts the story. He and his tiny kingdom of
Judah found themselves pressed into signing a treaty with the two
kingdoms that lay just north of his own: Israel and Aram (or Syria).
They wanted to form a three-nation alliance against Assyria.

Ahaz wasn't going to join the alliance. Israel and Aram were
threatening war.

In response, God sent a prophet to meet with Ahaz. His name
was Isaiah.

1. Peterson, *As Kingfishers Catch Fire*, 139.

2. Some may be more familiar with the initials BC, which stand for Before
Christ. The initials BCE stand for Before Common Era and these are more
regularly used today.

The prophet was told by God to take his son, Shear-Jashub, with him. A meeting of three: a prophet, a king, and a boy.

We don't know how old Isaiah's son was. Regardless, this boy journeyed with his father to remind the king of God's word. You see, this boy carried prophetic significance for the people of Judah. His name means "a remnant will return," which leaves both a flavor of promise and judgment in the mouth. Down the road, there would be disastrous destruction and exile. However, after a time of devastation, a remnant would return home. Still, it was only a remnant.

Not only would God communicate through the name of Isaiah's son, but the place where they would meet the king was also significant—the aqueduct of the Upper Pool (Isa 7:3). It was part of Ahaz's security arrangements against any impending siege.[3] God is going to speak to Ahaz in this meaningful place, reminding him that this aqueduct was not the protector. Instead, it was Yahweh who defends his people against any nation, whether small or large.[4]

Isaiah offered these four phrases to the king:

Be careful.

Keep calm.

Don't be afraid.

Do not lose heart.

A fitting message, noting their initial response: "the hearts of Ahaz and his people were shaken, as the trees of the forest are shaken by the wind" (Isa 7:2).

First off, we find a pastoral response in Isaiah's words. War is looming, but he says be careful, keep calm, don't be afraid, do not lose heart.

Moving through the story in Isaiah 7, God doesn't stop speaking. There is more. Through the prophet, God addresses Ahaz, telling him to ask for a *massive* sign, "whether in the deepest depths or in the highest heights" (Isa 7:11). As Eugene Peterson puts it, the king needs to, "Ask for the moon" (MSG).

3. Motyer, *The Prophecy of Isaiah*, 81.

4. This spelling, Yahweh, represents the most likely pronunciation of God's distinct and special name revealed to the Israelites.

Of course, Ahaz stiffens his back, straightens his collar, and then offers the most spiritual response he can drum up. At least it seems that way.

"I will not ask; I will not put the LORD to the test" (Isa 7:12). *Well done, Ahaz. Well done. Good answer!*

Or perhaps not.

Isaiah doesn't respond with a "well done." He reacts with anger. *Why is this king trying the patience of God?*

Don't let Ahaz's response fool you. He is an evil king. While all the kings in northern Israel were evil, at times a king in southern Judah might be good—or perhaps somewhere in the middle. Not with Ahaz. He was downright wicked. He made idols to worship other gods, sacrificed his son to those other gods, moved things around in the sacred temple without permission, and sent silver and gold to the pagan king of Assyria to sweet-talk him into relenting from any attack. You can read more in 2 Kings 16 and 2 Chronicles 28.

As I said, not good at all.

Yet God is exceptionally gracious here. Isaiah tells him that Israel and Aram will not be able to attack (Isa 7:7–9). And now God gently offers a gift to the king. Ask for a sign, and it can be as big as it needs to be.

When God offers us something, then perhaps it's okay to take him up on it.

Ahaz missed the most significant opportunity he may have ever had.

Isaiah continues in this vein: "Well, here's the thing. The Lord is going to give you a sign anyway, and this is what it will be: a virgin will give birth to a son and that son's name will be Immanuel."

Ah, there are those familiar words. And it would be easy in our minds to now run to the Gospel of Matthew for more insights. That may be our usual method, especially during the Advent season. The familiar draws us in.

Joseph.

Mary.

The angel.

The Holy Spirit.

The promise.

Immanuel.

God with us.

God physically *with us* in Jesus, the Messiah.

But perhaps we should stay in Isaiah 7 to navigate the original Immanuel account. I'm not sure we can adequately track with what's going on there. I've personally never been the king of a nation with war brewing in the background. But I want to try to feel a bit of the plot, to imagine what Ahaz is walking through. Remember, "the hearts of Ahaz and his people were shaken, as the trees of the forest are shaken by the wind" (Isa 7:2).

God is offering to protect his people in Judah, the house of David.

Israel, in the north, was already a defective people. Aram, just to the north of Israel, was outright pagan. Isaiah has told us those two kingdoms are going down. He also urges the king to stand firm in his faith, or he won't be able to stand at all (Isa 7:9).

With this background in mind, Isaiah tells Ahaz to ask for a sign, something that would *tangibly* remind him of God's promise. That's what signs are—distinct, concrete reminders of the promise of God. They are given to us to touch, hear, and see. At times, we may even smell and taste these signs, as we do at the Lord's Table.

However, as we have noted, Ahaz is not much interested in connecting with God. He's not going to stand firm in his faith; he's going to shun the opportunity of a lifetime.

"I won't ask," he declares.

Not even when it's okay to ask?

So, Isaiah tells him a boy of prophetic consequence is coming: "The virgin will conceive and give birth to a son, and will call him Immanuel" (Isa 7:14). We read about this child in the very next chapter, Isaiah 8. That boy's name? Maher-Shalal-Hash-Baz, which is just as prophetic as Isaiah's present son, Shear-Jashub.

This new boy's name means "quick to the plunder, swift to the spoil." A telling pointer of Israel's and Aram's future (Isa 8:4). We read just a bit earlier that these two lands will be laid waste (Isa 7:16). But here is the hard part to swallow for Ahaz and his people: a time of loss will also come for Judah (Isa 7:17-25).

Isaiah 7:14 and the sign of Immanuel take on a whole new meaning with this setting in mind. Isaiah has now moved to a place of "no longer persuading to faith but confirming divine displeasure."[5] A future enemy would one day ravage and ransack this people.

Immanuel, God with us.

The name that brings us deep comfort did not have the same effect for king Ahaz. For this king and his nation, the assurance of Immanuel was a mixed bag of promise and judgment.

This message isn't going to preach as well as we thought it would. It strips away any vision of Christmas sugarplums dancing in our heads.

Yet that is the text given to us in Isaiah. That's the story we must encounter.

It makes us want to rush to Matthew 1 even more quickly!

Still, perhaps we don't need to dodge this passage and all it has to offer. To wrestle with this ancient account may be what the doctor ordered.

Here we are reminded of the prophet's words to the king, and subsequently, his people: Yahweh, the one true God, was offering protection from the great terror that stood on their doorstep. That had been the people's story in the past. Remember Egypt? Remember the book of Judges? Encountering such nations would be their story for centuries to come.

Ahaz, stand firm in your faith, or you won't be able to stand.

Instead, Ahaz's faith would not flourish. He floundered by abandoning trust in and allegiance to his God. He rejected what the prophet had offered.

And this is where Immanuel comes in, not as an individual promise to just you or me. Instead, it is an assurance for God's collective people amid a challenging and changing landscape.

I recall an oft-quoted Psalm:

> Therefore we will not fear, though the earth give way
>   and the mountains fall into the heart of the sea,
> though its waters roar and foam
>   and the mountains quake with their surging. (Ps 46:2–3)

These words are the kind of language the Hebrews would use to portray turbulent changes taking place within their land. Many

---

5. Motyer, *The Prophecy of Isaiah*, 84.

times, the use of such imagery stood as verbal cues for describing deadly battle (see also Ps 46:9).

Threatening wars.

Shifting political landscapes.

The reminder rang forth: Ahaz's power rests not in allegiance to the nations surrounding him, but in loyal faith to Yahweh.

I am not suggesting any works-based plan to earn God's favor, just as Isaiah didn't offer any such system to Ahaz in his day. But I believe the original story of Immanuel reminds us that we find firm footing, not in alignment with the varying political powers that may be, whether in our own country or elsewhere. Instead, firm footing is found only in faithful allegiance to God, whom we now understand best through Jesus, the one true king.

This is the sign God has given us in Christ, the great Immanuel.

In Jesus's day, God's people also faced deep uncertainty across a history of national unrest.

Assyria in Ahaz's day.

Later on, Babylon.

Then Greece.

Rome in Jesus's time.

Centuries of disastrous unrest. Can you imagine? I know I can't.

Every Jew kept asking: *When will we be freed? When will we be delivered? Save us, O God!*

King Ahaz and the house of David asked these questions. The Jews of first-century Palestine did the same. A young woman conceived a son in Isaiah's day. A young virgin conceived a son some seven hundred years later.

Immanuel was promised in both settings.

Isaiah's words ended up as reproof to Ahaz, even as a remnant would arise out of a future catastrophe of that time. The words came to Mary with restorative hope: "He will save his people from their sins" (Matt 1:21). God's people would arise out of the tragedy of their day.

With the advent of Christ, the great Immanuel, we have God's enduring sign. Jesus has become the guarantor of a better covenant

(Heb 7:22). We can blossom out of the overflowing grace of God as we encounter our own adversity now and into the future.

Immanuel—then, now, and forever.

CHAPTER 2: THE ORIGINAL IMMANUEL

Questions for Reflection

1. In light of a fresh re-reading of Isaiah 7, what was most surprising to you about the passage? Were there any particular details not discussed in this book that you caught?

2. It is easy to read the Old Testament through the lens of the New Testament. And that is appropriate in light of Christ coming and now having the New Testament revelation. Yet, why might it be beneficial to understand the Old Testament accounts in their original context before considering how to read them in light of Christ and the New Testament?

3. Reflect on Jesus as God's great Immanuel. What are some of the ways in which he supersedes the practices and promises of the old covenant?

Chapter 3

A New Government

What Jews and Christians have in common—alone and with
no one else—is that we believe that there is one who is coming to make the world right.

–Walter Brueggemann[1]

I am going to go out on a limb here and speculate about something.
The word *government* tends to evoke all sorts of negative feelings in
us. For starters, there are the divisive, partisan politics around cru-
cial issues. We encounter too many politicians who have values but
very little virtue. Or perhaps the word calls to mind elections with
months and months of slanderous advertising and heated debates.
Toss in news pundits and social media interaction around political
issues, and it's no wonder some of us may have an aversion to the
word.

Knowing all this, it may be strange that, upon turning to a
well-known passage of Scripture, we twice come across the word
government in the span of just two verses.

> For to us a child is born,
>   to us a son is given,
>   and the government will be on his shoulders.
> And he will be called
>   Wonderful Counselor, Mighty God,

1. Brueggemann, *Celebrating Abundance*, 32.

Everlasting Father, Prince of Peace.
Of the greatness of his government and peace
    there will be no end.
He will reign on David's throne
    and over his kingdom,
establishing and upholding it
    with justice and righteousness
    from that time on and forever.
The zeal of the Lord Almighty
    will accomplish this. (Isa 9:6–7)

This particular Hebrew word for government [*misrah*], shows up only twice in the whole of the Old Testament. Both times are right here in Isaiah 9. Even with our English versions' use of the "g-word," it may be that this passage is relatively easy to swallow. There are some positives connected to what we find here:

1. We are told "the government will be on his shoulders," meaning it will be something that this child bears and commands. Not kings and politicians, but rather this special son.
2. Instead of chaos and turmoil, this government has justice, righteousness, and peace at its foundation.
3. The son in charge is identified by titles that, I think, draw us toward him: wonderful counselor, mighty God, everlasting father, prince of peace.

We can, perhaps, handle this kind of government, though there may still be trepidation.

But let's break this down a little more.

When we open the Bible and think about God being in charge, we may not think about government. We might instead visualize the idea of *kingdom*. Our Bibles use this term more regularly. Still, we can't forget that there are cultures in our world where the word *kingdom* is as distasteful for them as the word government is for us. Nevertheless, we believe God's kingdom is very much distinct from the governments—and kingdoms—of our world.

I would suggest that we discover the most meaningful insights about the kingdom of God when we head to the pages of the Gospels. We find out what this king is all about by listening to the words of Jesus and observing his actions. We walk away claiming, "Aha, that's what it's like when God is truly king, when he is in charge." Still, perhaps we find something similar right here in the words of Isaiah 9.

This little sermonette, however, does not begin with the famed Advent words of verses 6–7 in Isaiah 9. We need to head back to the first verse to understand the broader message. What we find may astound us:

No more gloom, but honor instead (Isa 9:1).

Light instead of darkness (Isa 9:2).

Enlarging and great rejoicing (Isa 9:3).

Burdens and oppression shattered (Isa 9:4).

The ending of war (Isa 9:5).

It is then that we fall upon the details of verses 6–7. Those earlier words set the scene for this new government.

What is most shocking is that the birth of a child will initiate everything about this government. For me, this brings to mind the original Immanuel promise back in Isaiah 7, which we discussed in the last chapter. Now the assurance comes that this little child will launch a new kind of rule.

What is God's deal with using children? I don't mean in just a few places, but throughout Scripture. Children were significant in the ancient world, as was land. Extremely important! They constituted the continuance of a family's lineage and the passing on of one's inheritance. The inheritance was usually passed to the firstborn male. For Abraham to not have offspring was a significant predicament in the minds of the ancients. And the more children, the merrier.

For Isaiah to again tell the people that a child, particularly a son, would be born, would have been music to the ears of the ancient Israelites. It would have grabbed their attention.

A child initiates the kingdom and, recalling the words of Jesus, it is the childlike who enter God's kingdom (Matt 18:3).

Again, God and children. There's something in this here.

Who's this new boy going to be? What's this new son going to do?

This new king that Isaiah tells us about is going to carry unique titles, as noted above. The designations given to the son are unlike any before him.

This government is not one *they* had known.

This government is not one *we* have known.

But this is the government of God: the good, right, and just kingdom of God that would come forth through the son-to-be-born, God with us, Immanuel. This government—one of wonderful counsel, strength, and might, a fatherly heart, and *shalom*-peace—is one of which we want to be part. I know I do.

This kingdom is sure and right because it rests on the son's shoulders. We discover confidence when we see that the way of peace will increase in abundance. There will be no end to this good king and his kingdom.

But we are also told he's going to sit on David's throne.

If this passage is ultimately talking about Jesus's kingdom, then why bring up David?

David is hugely important in the Bible, primarily because the Bible is a Jewish story. And David was the pinnacle king in their account. Not only that, but the prophets continue to tell the story that someone like David is coming to be king. At times, it seems like they announce David himself will return—consider passages like Ezekiel 34:23–24 and 37:24–25.

I don't believe they thought that David would return in the flesh, resurrection-style, but only that someone *from the line of David* would be seated on his throne. Remember, the ancients held up family lineage as extremely important. The future ruler would need to connect to the past kings, especially the greatest one, David.

So, the question begs itself: Has this son, this king, been seated on David's throne?

In the last chapter, I did not want to rush ahead when working through the Immanuel promise of Isaiah 7. In this chapter, I want to peek in on a future sermon that may help us with Isaiah 9. This is not a homily from our time, but rather Peter's first public speech since Christ's ascension, found in Acts 2.

We undoubtedly remember the account of Pentecost reported by Luke. A strong rushing wind, tongues of fire resting on the disciples. These followers of Jesus begin speaking different languages, ones they had not learned (Acts 2:2–4).

For this occasion, there was a multitude of Jews from outside the holy land who had journeyed to Jerusalem. They were there for the Feast of Pentecost (Acts 2:5). This was not the first time this special feast had taken place. It was an annual celebration the Jews called Shavuot. God's people would make a pilgrimage to Jerusalem to engage in a week-long festival. As Americans, we know how to *party* for a few hours and then head back home. The ancients knew how to truly *celebrate*. For Shavuot, an entire week was filled with eating and drinking, worship and celebration, recreation and rest!

The visitors to Jerusalem were blown away by what they had both seen and heard. They were taken aback in hearing folk speak in their native language (Acts 2:6).

How do they know our language?

I imagine the visitors knew these local disciples had not originally spoken these languages, mainly due to the accents detected. I remember when I first began learning Dutch (or Flemish, as it's called in Belgium). It was difficult to drop my American accent.

Many gathered at Pentecost were asking, "What in the world does this event mean?!"

Others replied, "They're only drunk!"

During all the confusion, Peter stood, raised his voice, and offered insights into what has just happened:

"They are not drunk!"—as if one suddenly learns another language by getting drunk!—"Instead, somebody a long time ago told us this would happen" (Acts 2:15–16, my paraphrase).

Peter proceeds to quote the old prophet Joel, particularly his words about something astonishing that would take place in the last days. The Spirit would be poured out: prophecy, visions, and dreams would become a reality. It would involve both men and women, young and old—all types of people (Acts 2:17–18).

Not only that, but a cataclysmic shift would take place in such a way that the ancient prophet Joel would describe it with evocative, poetic license. Blood, fire, billows of smoke. The sun would stop shining, and the moon would turn blood red (Joel 2:19–20).

Yikes!

The Jews would not have looked to the skies to see if things were suddenly happening in the cosmos. They did not expect the sun's light to fade out. They were not looking for an amber-red moon. Instead, they understood that Joel—and now Peter—was describing a momentous change that would take place.

Peter is essentially saying, "What you have just seen and heard signifies that the last days have arrived. God is judging an old order, and it's coming to an end. The future is arriving, and it is even beginning today. It is time for God's Messiah to be in charge."

And how do we know this?

"By the Spirit being poured out on all peoples," Peter would reply. "Remember, Joel said all of this long ago."

But Joel's words do not say anything about Jesus being in charge, right?

Like any good preacher, Peter continues with more.

He then quotes from Psalm 16, a song-prayer of David (see Acts 2:25–28). God would not abandon to the grave his anointed, set-apart one. The place of death would not be the final destination for God's Son.

Peter resumes, reminding them that David had died. But David was a prophet and spoke of one of his descendants who would be seated on his throne (Acts 2:29–30).

Who's throne?

David's throne.

Pause and recall Isaiah 9.

The one whose peaceful reign would increase—that son was going to sit on David's throne and reign over his kingdom.

Back to Peter and Acts 2.

"But he [David] was a prophet and knew that God had promised him on oath that he would place one of his descendants on his throne" (Acts 2:30).

How would this descendant be placed on David's throne—and subsequently reign over his kingdom?

Through resurrection. That's what Peter wants the onlookers, and us, to know.

To sum up, Peter is telling those present at the Feast of Pentecost (or Shavuot) that, in Psalm 16, David received a promise. It started with him, but David knew death would come. Still, he saw what was to come. As a prophet, he also knew that God was promising to seat one of his descendants on his throne (Acts 2:30). God would not forsake his holy one in the grave, and David's heir would be seated on David's throne through the resurrection of the Messiah, who is Jesus (Acts 2:31).

But here is the kicker. Jerusalem was no longer the center of this kingdom. This throne of David was now at the right hand of the Father (Acts 2:33). David's son would then rule over all nations!

Peter's concluding statement: "Therefore let all Israel be assured of this: God has made this Jesus, whom you crucified, both Lord and Messiah" (Acts 2:36). He is the anointed king. He is in charge.

Again, how do we know that Jesus is in charge—other than from Peter's own message?

God would pour out the Holy Spirit (Acts 2:33). They had all just visually and audibly witnessed this amidst their festive celebrations!

A child was going to be born, one in which the government of God would rest on his shoulders. He would be a wonderful counselor, mighty God, everlasting father, prince of peace (Isa 9:6). This king would lead a kingdom of true justice and righteousness, one like they had never known. This son would be required to sit on David's throne and rule over David's kingdom. Peter tells us this has now taken place. The last days have come—the old Jewish system has been judged and found wanting. A new era has emerged. The Messiah is now in charge. He rules over all nations. The Spirit of God is poured out on all flesh.

David's son is here.

David's son is in charge.

That's good news.

This good news changed things then, and it certainly changes things now. The promised son would make the world right. Things would be shaped as God always intended. We aren't there yet.

Not entirely, at least. But we are on our way. The mustard seed is growing.

> For to us a child is born,
>> to us a son is given,
>> and the government will be on his shoulders. (Isa 9:6)

This new government, this new kingdom of the son, calls to us. And this call, this expectation for a new kingdom, is the theme of the Advent season.

CHAPTER 3: A NEW GOVERNMENT

Questions for Reflection

1. Re-read Isaiah 9:1–7. In the passage, we read of many things that will take place because of the son that would be born. Which aspects stand out to you, and why?
2. What might it look like for God's people, the church, to live in light of a king and kingdom described in such a way as found in verses 6–7? In view of these verses, is there anything that needs to change for the church in our society today?

CHAPTER 4

Job (the guy in the Bible)

To be human is to be in trouble.

−EUGENE PETERSON[1]

Matthew, Luke, and Isaiah. As we've noted, these are the usual suspects in a line-up of Advent and Christmas sermons. However, one place the church will probably not turn to is the book of Job.

Of course not. How does that book even relate to the season?

I want to offer a reflection of why the words of Job just might be a place we should turn during the Advent season.

In seminary, I learned that the book of Job (along with Ecclesiastes) fell into the category of "contemplative wisdom literature." Whereas the words of Proverbs seemed straightforward—and if you obeyed them, the outcome seemed straightforward as well—Job was not so tidy. There was no such equation to follow: do A (be good) and it will lead to B (blessings).

Yet, here's the thing. Job's life pretty much lined up with the wise instruction found in the Old Testament, especially in places like Proverbs. However, the result did not look like what the book of Proverbs seemed to have promised.[2]

1. Peterson, *A Long Obedience in the Same Direction*, 137.

2. I am aware that Job might have been, probably was, written well before the collection of Proverbs. I am using a bit of tongue-in-cheek humor to make the point.

That's just it. While Proverbs offers wisdom, it does so in generalized, brief bursts. The statements are not the be-all, end-all of life. That's because a short, oversimplified blast of wisdom does not allow all aspects of life to be considered.

It's not unlike modern-day proverbs. For example, "An apple a day keeps the doctor away." The *general* thrust behind this statement is that eating fruit (or eating nutritious foods) keeps you in good health, curbing multiple doctor visits due to illness.

Well, that's all fine and dandy. But there are plenty of people who disprove this apple adage. For starters, some do not choose to eat healthily, yet they are doing just fine. Some eat reasonably well, but a healthy diet, some may point out, is no guarantor of a long and healthy life. Terrible illnesses and accidents still happen.

In some instances, an apple a day does not keep the doctor away.

Do you see the disparity between a brief statement of general wisdom and real life?

The book of Proverbs is wonderful, no doubt. But you cannot "name it and claim it" using a verse out of Proverbs. No single proverb considers all facets of life.

For example, note these well-known words in Proverbs 22:6:

> Start children off on the way they should go,
>   and even when they are old they will not turn from it.

Some may be more familiar with other translations that begin with the words, "Train up a child in the way he should go."

Of course, we want to start children off—or train them up—on the proper path. And we anticipate that they will stay on that track. But there are a host of factors at play: friends and school, jobs and hobbies, social media and the internet, and so on. There are so many dynamics at play in this world, including a person's will and choice.

That's where Job (and Ecclesiastes) comes in. It offers a wise and careful reflection on life, reminding us that we are not entirely sure why such and such is taking place. We are not always privy as to why certain things happen to us in the way they do.

Job's life lined up with Proverbs. That was part of Job's argument to his three friends—"I've not done anything wrong!" Scripture itself tells us that Job had not sinned (see Job 1:22; 2:10; 42:7).

Again, his life lined up with the righteous way. But his circumstances *appeared* as if he had been engaging in wickedness.

How this truly relates to life today.

Here is something we must also remember about the book of Job: we are privy to the opening scene of chapters 1 and 2, something both Job and his friends were not. We enter the story from a different perspective than Job. He is trying to wrap his head around what has happened. Why have circumstances of such tragic proportions come upon him and his family?

His friends remind him of the general prudence about how life works. They assume the conditions of life always correspond to one's actions: wisdom with which all the ancients would agree.

But it does not fit Job's story.

Instead, this poor man is somehow learning that wisdom can be painful and prolonged. It develops over time and even through tragedy. Microwaves cannot zap this.

I hope we are beginning to glimpse how the wisdom of Job is very different from Proverbs.

Now, what does all of this have to do with Advent?

Historically, Advent has been a time of preparation, a period of anticipating the arrival of the Christ-child. Yet, this hopeful expectation also couples with genuine, painful reflection.

In the time leading up to Jesus's birth, the people of God had been lamenting their socio-political situation. Why so? The reality of oppression, the lack of liberation. As we've seen previously, it had been Egypt, then Assyria, next Babylon, and on to Persia. The period between the Old and New Testaments had the Greeks followed by the Ptolemies and Seleucids. A litany of oppressors!

Now it was Rome.

The setting Jesus stepped into was a mess—politically, religiously, and socially.

In the few centuries leading up to Jesus's birth, there were whispers (or proclamations) of a special one to come.[3] Excitement rose in the blood of the Jews as Judas Maccabeus took down Antiochus IV and the oppressive Seleucid rule.[4] But it always came back to the same reality: things were just not right. Life was not the way it was supposed to be. Another world power would simply step in and squash any attempt by this little Jewish nation to become anything of substance.

Lament.

Pain.

Tears.

Disappointment.

Anger.

Not just individually, but collectively as well.

God, when will you come through? When will you send your Messiah, the deliverer we've been hearing about for centuries now?

Hundreds of years.

That's a long time to wait.

That's a long time to anticipate.

That's a long time to feel your pain. That's a lengthy period to lament and cry.

The Jews would have had questions too numerous to count!

As with the Jews long, painful wait for God's Messiah to come, Job reminds us that it is okay to lament, be angry, question, and dialogue honestly with God, even if he remains quiet. I imagine the Jews of Jesus's day were used to hearing that pin drop, wondering when God would speak.

We could say our world today is in tumultuous upheaval.

Another school shooting.

Another injustice toward a minority.

Another baby dismembered.

Another terrorist opens fire.

Another suicide.

3. Most notably in the Jewish writings of Wisdom and Sirach, found in the Apocrypha.

4. You can read about this in First Maccabees, which is also included in the Apocrypha.

Another election.

Another friend's betrayal.

Another failure in loving spouse and children.

Another virus spreads.

So much pain and agony. So many questions.

Why won't things change?

In those times, we would do well to allow Job to become our mentor, to draw close into his bosom of wisdom. Perhaps if we listen, we can learn much from his plight.

Yet, the book of Job does not stop there. Nor does our Advent anticipation. We turn to the final chapter, the epilogue of Job, and we read that God both vindicates and restores Job.

Yes!

A poetic drama played out at a sluggish pace of forty-two chapters.

How much back and forth can he endure?

But the wait is well worth it. Those last eleven verses of chapter 42 are a cup of cold water for a parched mouth. We are ready to join the chorus of hallelujahs! Or perhaps we're too exhausted.

God's people of old waited through centuries of agony and frustration. Facing exile, war, and loss of sacred space and land, it seems they were always under the control of one hostile power or another.

Then a baby is born.

A king, a Messiah, a deliverer. He announces a good news message, a proclamation that God's kingdom was arriving.

Redemption had come at last.

The ache was over.

And here we are now, ourselves, preparing to enter another season of Advent. We await the arrival of the Christ-child in the church calendar. We also anticipate a second Advent when Jesus will completely renew all things. It will be a time of singing the well-known refrain: *He will wipe every tear from their eyes. There will be no more death or mourning or crying or pain, for the old order of things has passed away* (Rev 21:4). It will be a world with a river of living water and healing leaves with no more curse and no more night (Rev 22:1–5).

But tears, death, and mourning are still present today.

We are anticipating Christ's arrival. We are awaiting Christ's coming in the future.

Job has something to teach us during Advent—both in our seasons of pain and in our seasons of hope as God's people.

Painful reflection.

Promising hope.

Perhaps we will read Job's story this Advent.

CHAPTER 4: JOB (THE GUY IN THE BIBLE)

Questions for Reflection

1. Have you ever been able to read the story of Job in the Bible? Consider reading it with a newer translation such as the Common English Bible or The Message. In particular, read chapters 1–3 to get a glimpse into Job's pain. What catches your attention most about both Job's circumstances (Job 1–2) and his response (Job 3)?

2. Read Job 3:25–26. Do you feel your circumstances are similar, having no peace or rest, only knowing turmoil? If you are personally in a season of deep anguish, what might be the very next step to take? Who might be able to help you take that next step?

CHAPTER 5

Lament in Advent

Some Christians tend to pray to God as if we can hide from
him what's really going on in our minds. We should be honest
with God if we're impatient with him or angry with him or
disappointed with him. We certainly won't fool him if we
bottle it up inside.

–TREMPER LONGMAN[1]

The Bible is a collection of all kinds of literature. From narrative accounts to songs to parables to prayers. There are letters, commands, allegories, and dramatic plays. Not to mention visions, prophecies, and poems. The church believes that God was not afraid to speak in numerous ways across varying literary styles.

Some of these are much easier to grapple with (perhaps the letters and prayers). Others, not so much (like prophecies and visions).

One of the places where we turn to most in the Bible is the Psalms. They were the songs and prayers of the ancient Hebrews. These songlike poems draw us in, I believe, because of their honest and expressive heart. That allows them to connect with our own emotions deeply. While we may not understand all the ins and outs of Hebrew parallelism,[2] this old worship book is much more

1. Longman, *How to Read the Psalms*, 135.

2. The Hebrews primarily used the literary device of parallelism when writing their poetry. In this style, a statement would be made in one line (i.e.,

accessible than the sharp commands of the Law, the bloody narratives of Judges and Kings, and the obscure visions of the Prophets.

We may not all be poets, but for many, the lyrical prayers of the Psalms uniquely call to each of us. Tremper Longman states it plainly: "Poems appeal to the whole person in a way that prose does not."[3] The poetic portions of Scripture, with the Psalms as their apex, call to the deep recesses of our being. They are the place we head to in remarkable moments of joy and gratitude, as well as our darkest moments of despair and pain—not to mention everywhere else in between. They might just be the place to which we turn in Scripture when we know of nowhere else to turn.

The Psalms are certainly the place where the Hebrews would go to find words to assign to their emotions and heartfelt prayers. With that, they would have undoubtedly understood the laments, which served as the struggling questions and cries of God's people. Interestingly, lament happens to make up the most substantial portion of the Psalms. There are far more expressions of lamentation than there are of exuberant praise. They are the songs and prayers, literally the complaints, in which the writers held nothing back in expressing their hurt, frustration, confusion, despair, and more.

The psalmists would express a lament for three central reasons:[4]

1. They are troubled by their own thoughts.
2. They are troubled by others' actions against them.
3. They are troubled by God himself.

The first two seem acceptable, perhaps, but are we sure about the last? Upset with God? But that's just what we find amongst the psalmists' groanings:

> Why, Lord, do you stand far off?
> Why do you hide yourself in times of trouble? (Ps 10:1)

---

first half of a verse) and then in the very next line (i.e., second half of a verse) that statement would be carried forward in a similar, yet distinct, way.

3. Longman, *How to Read the Psalms*, 91.

4. I am grateful for Longman simplifying this in *How to Read the Psalms*, 26.

How long, Lord? Will you forget me forever?
How long will you hide your face from me? (Ps 13:1)

They do not sound like your average prayer or song lyric in our churches today. Yet, that is what we find amidst the pages of holy Scripture. Raw honesty. The beginning words of Psalm 22 are candid:

My God, my God, why have you forsaken me?
Why are you so far from saving me,
so far from my cries of anguish?
My God, I cry out by day, but you do not answer,
by night, but I find no rest. (Ps 22:1–2)

Remember, these are the words Jesus declares from the cross. *Can Jesus say those kinds of things?*
I think so.
But why all this theology about the Psalms? I thought we were talking about Advent here.
That's just it. In many ways, Advent is that time where we long for God to come through for us. It is the space of tension that exists between longing and frustration, expectation and confusion, hope and despair. And sometimes we find ourselves leaning into the pain over the promise. Remember Job in the previous chapter? That's life; that's reality—for those in Bible times and us.
Fittingly, we should find solace in turning to the Psalms to discover ways to voice our anger and hurt, fears and loneliness, sadness and anxiety. Some of us are in desperate times. We are yearning for God to come through. And the wait we have encountered has extended well past its welcome.
The psalmists knew this. The ancients were acquainted with grief just as we are. And their laments and complaints made it straight into the inspired Bible itself.
As we move across the pages of the Psalms, we notice things we may not have seen before: questions, cries, and even judgmental cursings. We were perhaps frightened that our hearts were in the wrong, or, worse yet, dead. But the Psalms remind us that our hearts are still beating.

Heading to these ancient prayers, with our emotions at the forefront, we begin to notice things we had not seen previously.

> As the deer pants for streams of water,
>   so my soul pants for you, my God.
> My soul thirsts for God, for the living God.
>   When can I go and meet with God?
> My tears have been my food
>   day and night,
> while people say to me all day long,
>   "Where is your God?" (Ps 42:1–3)

With this particular psalm, we typically stop at verse 2. Thus, we see this prayer as someone engaged in a passionately, intimate worship session. But verse 3 makes it very clear that these words are not describing what we had first thought. Things are so bad, so terrible that *their tears have been their food day and night*. The psalmist is crying so much that their tears have turned into their food.

What an image!

But that's our story as well. It precisely describes what we have experienced or are currently experiencing. We can't even think of putting two pieces of bread together for a meal. Our salt-laden tears are all we taste.

Here are some more gut-wrenching words of David:

> Even my close friend,
>   someone I trusted,
> one who shared my bread,
>   has turned against me. (Ps 41:9)

Betrayal was real then, and it is real now. Jesus himself would employ these words centuries later at a table with his close friends. The betrayal of Judas would lead him to echo these words. Perhaps Jesus ended up crying out those words that we examined from Psalm 42: "My tears have been my food day and night." We can only imagine what the Garden of Gethsemane was like for Christ.

If the saints of old could feel it and pray it, then how about us? If Jesus could feel it and pray it, then why not you and me? These were their laments; these are our laments.

And, so, Advent reminds us that it is okay—no, that it is *necessary*—to enter our pain and voice the anguish. Or, if we don't, as Chip Dodd reminds us, "Either you deal with your heart, or the attempts to stop your heart's voice will create such conflict that it will break your life into pieces."[5]

We all have wounds from living in this world. We have a lot to lament these days.

Betrayals. Job loss. Dissolved marriages. Addictions.

Sexual abuse. Politics. Poverty. Hunger. Pandemics.

So much to lament.

And sometimes, we need to embrace our loss with intentionality, navigate our pain with care, and become acquainted with our griefs with honesty.

Will we sit and listen—if only to our own hearts?

Then we might know how to give voice to what is going on. We may be able to express our emotions just as the psalmist did long ago.

I understand that lament may seem more in line with the season of Lent than Advent. Isn't Advent more about joyous expectation? But recalling the Jews' painful plight, under the constant rule of evil empires as they yearned for and awaited the coming Messiah, the season of Advent also gives us permission to feel our own sorrow and grief as we even now long for Jesus's final coming to renew our world.

Immanuel, God with us, steps into our pain. Many times, we do not sense it. But he remains Immanuel. And, in this, he offers us the gift of lament as we long for his coming during the season of Advent.

---

5. Dodd, *The Voice of the Heart*, 14.

CHAPTER 5: LAMENT IN ADVENT

Questions for Reflection

1. Does it shock you at times to consider the honest and painful expressions within the Psalms? Why or why not?

2. In your current life situation, what may be causing you to feel hurt, frustrated, anxious, or angry? Is there a lament psalm you could turn to that may be able to help voice what you are feeling? If so, consider slowly reading that psalm and turning it into a prayer. If you do not have a specific psalm of lament in mind, consider turning to one of these: 5, 6, 13, 28, 31, 38, 43, 51, 61, 80, 120, or 130.

CHAPTER 6

Waiting and Hoping

...for Jesus ... there is no conceptual differentiation between
waiting and hoping. They are one and the same activity.

−K.C. IRETON[1]

We don't usually like to wait. And that may be putting it lightly. We
avoid lines at all costs, sometimes even preordering our lattes via
smartphone apps and having our groceries delivered straight to our
doors. Of course, we have developed an affinity for *fast* food.

As I said, we are not prone to waiting.

But waiting is a part of life. Benjamin Franklin once remarked
that there are two certainties in life: death and taxes. Perhaps we
could add a third: waiting.

Waiting *in* traffic. Waiting *on* a friend. Waiting *to* go home
from work. Waiting *for* summer vacation.

Waiting *in* the doctor's office. Waiting *on* the school bell to
ring. Waiting *to* receive a package. Waiting *for* the weekend.

It is a big chunk of life, from the cradle to the grave. If this is
true, it may do us well to come to terms with the inevitability of our
waiting.

Heading back into the Psalms, we read of the ancient Hebrews'
expressions of waiting.

---

1. Ireton, *The Circle of Seasons*, 24.

Wait for the LORD;
>be strong and take heart
>and wait for the LORD. (Ps 27:14, emphasis mine)

I *waited* patiently for the LORD;
>he turned to me and heard my cry.
He lifted me out of the slimy pit,
>out of the mud and mire;
he set my feet on a rock
>and gave me a firm place to stand.
He put a new song in my mouth,
>a hymn of praise to our God.
Many will see and fear the LORD
>and put their trust in him. (Ps 40:1–3, emphasis mine)

I *wait* for the LORD, my whole being *waits*,
>and in his word I put my hope.
I *wait* for the LORD
>more than watchmen wait for the morning,
>more than watchmen wait for the morning. (Ps 130:5–6, emphasis mine)

The Hebrew word used in these passages for "wait" is *qavah*. Whereas for us, waiting commonly carries a sense of annoyance, it was a more expectant—even hopeful—word for the ancients. That is why the Hebrew word can be translated with the phrase *hope in* rather than *wait for*. The Common English Bible (CEB) is one translation that does this.

In the previous chapter, we looked at the reality of the lament. We observed an overabundance of these types of prayers and songs where the psalmists pour out their hurt, frustration, confusion, despair, and more.

However, what you will always find within laments is a nugget of hope and promise. Things were terrible; life was devastating; the writers were in the lowest dumps of despair. Yet, there was some sense of hopeful anticipation, even if only a smidgen.

That is what their waiting involved: anticipatory hope. Not a happy-clappy, smoothing-over-the-problems-of-life false hope. Rather, it was one sincerely rooted in God.

When we speak of hope today, it carries a sense of uncertainty:

I hope everything turns out okay.

I hope I get a raise.

I hope I make the team.

These expressions sound more like an "I don't know" than statements of expectancy.

Please hear me: I am not negating the genuineness of lament, ache, uncertainty, or questions. By no means! That is why I explored what I did in the last chapter and illustrated why such is a right—and godly—practice. The "Why, Lord?" and "Where are you, God?" must be articulated, lest we become crushed under the pretense of a false religion.

But our questions and pain—our waiting—do not end there. It did not stop there for the psalmists, and it does not stop there for us either. Or it does not have to.

We painstakingly long for God to come through. That's what we observed just above in the words of Psalm 130, as the writer voiced, "my whole being waits" (Ps 130:5). This expression here uses the Hebrew word for soul [*nephesh*]. The psalmist is suggesting that their wait involves *all* that is in them. We would imagine such when we see how the prayer begins:

> *Out of the depths I cry to you, LORD;*
>   LORD, hear my voice.
> Let your ears be attentive
>   to my cry for mercy. (Ps 130:1, emphasis mine)

So, as we've noted, within each of these distressing cries, we will uncover some sense of hope. It may only seem a drop, but it is there.

Let's revisit some of the psalms we considered in the preceding chapter and dive into a bit more of the context:

> But you, God, see the trouble of the afflicted;
>   you consider their grief and take it in hand.
> The victims commit themselves to you;
>   you are the helper of the fatherless . . .
> You, LORD, hear the desire of the afflicted;
>   you encourage them, and you listen to their cry,

defending the fatherless and the oppressed,
    so that mere earthly mortals
    will never again strike terror. (Ps 10:14, 17–18)

But I trust in your unfailing love;
    my heart rejoices in your salvation.
I will sing the LORD's praise,
    for he has been good to me. (Ps 13:5–6)

For he has not despised or scorned
    the suffering of the afflicted one;
he has not hidden his face from him
    but has listened to his cry for help. (Ps 22:24)

Israel, put your hope in the LORD,
    for with the LORD is unfailing love
    and with him is full redemption.
He himself will redeem Israel
    from all their sins. (Ps 130:7–8)

The psalmists were brutally honest at times about their situations. Yet, somehow, amid the sorrow and suffering, they recalled their hope in God. They were waiting for—hopefully anticipating—God to do something real and tangible in their midst. The devastating situations of life moved their soul to cry out in confusion and anger. Still, they anchored their hope and waiting in God, both in who he was and what he would do. Not a false hope, but one rooted and established in the eternally faithful God.

Of course, when God answered the lament, the psalmist would turn around with a song and prayer of profound gratitude. In his book on the Psalms, Tremper Longman notes that an essential characteristic that sets Christians apart is that we are a people who *give thanks.*[2] Gratefulness is not some cheesy, pious notion. Instead, it is our real response that springs forth as we have come through agonizingly painful realities. Anyone who has gone through such—and come out on the other side—knows of what I speak.

---

2. Longman, *How to Read the Psalms*, 143–44.

And the magnitude of our gratefulness is typically tied to the length of waiting on, or hoping in, God. I think we know that one as well.

Tying this into Advent, we have to consider just *how long* God's people had been waiting for the Messiah. Not days, not weeks, not months, not years. Not even decades upon decades of waiting and hoping. We are talking about centuries and centuries here.

Then that first announcement of the angel rang forth: The Messiah was coming, and God would rescue his people! So, guess what happened? Amongst many things, a song of worship and gratitude spilled forth from the lips of Mary, the Messiah's mother:

> My soul glorifies the Lord
> > and my spirit rejoices in God my Savior,
> for he has been mindful
> > of the humble state of his servant.
> From now on all generations will call me blessed,
> > for the Mighty One has done great things for me—
> > holy is his name.
> His mercy extends to those who fear him,
> > from generation to generation.
> He has performed mighty deeds with his arm;
> > he has scattered those who are proud in their inmost
> > thoughts.
> He has brought down rulers from their thrones
> > but has lifted up the humble.
> He has filled the hungry with good things
> > but has sent the rich away empty.
> He has helped his servant Israel,
> > remembering to be merciful
> to Abraham and his descendants forever,
> > just as he promised our ancestors. (Luke 1:46–55)

Finally, Immanuel has come! Our wait has come to an end. Our hope has found its resolution. Immanuel: God was now with us in Christ.

CHAPTER 6: WAITING AND HOPING

Questions for Reflection

1. What are you currently waiting on—or hoping for—with God? How long has the wait lasted?
2. Is there a particular psalm you could read and return to regularly during this time of waiting and hoping? Perhaps consider Psalm 40 or 130. Or you could do an online search for "wait" or "hope" to find a psalm that may be more appropriate for you.
3. Has there been something you were waiting on in the past, and God came through with an answer? What is it?
4. How were you able to express your gratefulness to God and celebrate God's provision for the answer?

CHAPTER 7

The Forerunner

The announcement of John's birth has thus provided the occasion for an even more astounding proclamation. The period
of waiting is drawing to a close. God is on the move. Final
preparations are necessary, and John will have the central,
prophetic role in proclaiming the looming advent of the Lord.

−JOEL GREEN[1]

Soon after opening his Gospel account, Luke launches into a story.
Whereas Matthew leads with a genealogy, followed by a narrative
about Christ, Luke starts with the forerunner. Mark had done this
as well, but Luke adds in many more family details to his account.

That forerunner is known as John the Baptizer. While Mark
describes him in the vein of the ancient prophets of Israel (see Mark
1:4–6)—perhaps stirring up images of a Hagrid-like figure from the
Harry Potter series—Luke lets us peer into the family of John.

His parents both come from a priestly background and have
lived impeccable lives of righteousness (Luke 1:5–6). Zechariah and
Elizabeth were exemplary Jews, we might say. However, as in the
manner of some renowned Jewish women before her, Elizabeth has
found herself childless. A reasonably weighty affliction upon a married woman in the ancient world. She undoubtedly had spent time

1. Green, *The Gospel of Luke*, 78.

rehashing the stories of Sarah, Hannah, and the like as she cried out to God in one of those prayerful laments.

Whenever we come across an account in Scripture in which we encounter a woman who has remained childless for quite some time, you can likely expect that something significant is about to take place. A child will come forth, and that child will have a meaningful role to play for God's people. And such was the case with Elizabeth and her son, John.

Zechariah, the husband, had been called to his priestly service (Luke 1:8–9). The lot had determined his time for a particular duty. Casting lots was a way the ancients ensured the choice was not human but rather divine. Accordingly, as Joel Green notes, when the early Christian disciples read Luke's unfolding account, they would have sensed a profound sacredness in the story.[2]

A priest.

In the temple.

Chosen by lot.

Burning of incense at the altar.

The above describes a scene of solemn expectation. In this holiest of moments, the angel Gabriel arrives. As the angel appears to Zechariah, we find him responding in precisely the same manner as just about everyone else in the Bible—shock and fear (Luke 1:12). So, Gabriel has to follow up with the customary angelic reply: "Do not be afraid" (Luke 1:13).

Easier said than done, right?

But Gabriel continues, and with good news.

"Your prayer has been heard" (Luke 1:13).

We know the prayer of which the angel speaks. Very different from Joseph and Mary, Zechariah and Elizabeth had been praying to receive such a gift for who knows how long. Their story echoes that of Abraham and Sarah, seen through Zechariah's words, "I am an old man and my wife is well along in years" (Luke 1:18).

Let's hold on some of the details for now about this soon-to-be-born child. First, let's consider Zechariah's reaction and his dilemma in light of that response. I imagine his reply is not unlike

---

2. Green, *The Gospel of Luke*, 70.

what my own would have been at that moment. I would like to believe that my answer would be one of unwavering resolve, but how does one respond during their first encounter with an angel? At the very least, his reaction parallels many who have gone before him, struggling to believe God's promise—even when it is the angel of the Lord who has delivered it. Again, the Jewish mind would recall the father and mother of their faith, Abraham and Sarah.

On this occasion, because of his inability to take Gabriel at his word, Zechariah is told that he will be unable to speak until his son is born (Luke 1:20). Of course, there is plenty written about the benefit of silence as a gift in our journey with God. Coupled with solitude, they become a source in which, as Richard Foster reminds us, we learn to truly "see and hear."[3] But in Zechariah's case, the silence serves as a reprimand rather than a gift.

And this is going to last a full nine months. Ouch!

The question indeed arises: Why so harsh, Gabriel? Others have responded in the same way as Zechariah. Perhaps even Mary herself seems to struggle with the angel's words, as seen just a few verses later (see her question in verse 34).

Here is my hunch as to what may be going on. God is about to do something through the birth of this little boy. And it was Zechariah's silence, along with his future speaking and singing, that would highlight the divinely appointed nature of John's name and call.

Stay with me for a moment.

Later on, once this new baby boy was born, a significant group of family and friends were present (Luke 1:58–59). And when it was time to name the child, accurate to any community gathering, they felt the need to chime in with their insights. The expectation was that the baby would be named after his father. It at least made sense to them.

However, Elizabeth offers a different name. She throws a curveball, if you will.

"He is to be called John" (Luke 1:60).

---

3. Foster, *Celebration of Discipline*, 98.

"No, no, no," comes the criticism from the nearby support team! "No one else in the family has that name" (Luke 1:61). They, then, turn to the father to straighten things out. He can't talk, but perhaps they can find another way for him to communicate.

Zechariah calls for a notepad of sorts and a writing utensil, scribbles down a few words, and then turns the tablet back toward the gathered crowd to reveal a name. They step back, astonished. He has reported just as Elizabeth had—"His name is John" (Luke 1:63).

It is at that moment that the period of silence expires for Zechariah (Luke 1:64). Perhaps there was some kind of tingle within his mouth to let him know. Who knows? But all he could do was offer praise to God—for his voice returning and the birth of his son. Moreover, Zechariah is about to burst forth with a Spirit-filled, prophetic song.

So, we come to John's name.

It means "God is gracious." And he has indeed shown favor to Elizabeth, taking away her *dis-grace* (Luke 1:25). Yet, through this boy, God will display his generous grace to his entire people, which is what Zechariah's song gets at. Take a look at the lyrical content in verses 68–79!

Redemption.

Salvation.

Deliverance from enemies.

Mercy.

Remembering his covenant promise.

A renewed ability to serve God.

Forgiveness of sin.

Tender mercy.

Light shining in darkness.

Peace.

It sounds as if this is something to be sung about Jesus. The thing is, they are words that connect to Christ and what he would do. Zechariah's boy shall be the forerunner to the coming Messiah. His life will, in many ways, echo that of Jesus. He has come to "prepare the way" for the Messiah.

To end, I want to return to Gabriel's earlier message to Zechariah to help us think through part of John's calling. It was unique, especially given that this boy was filled with the Spirit before birth. *What does that even look like?* This exceptional work of the Spirit appears to speak to John's prophetic role, even before he is born, as seen later with Elizabeth's visit to Mary (Luke 1:39–45).[4]

Yet, more importantly, I offer that the angel's words about John are formative for the people of God today, especially as seen in verses 16–17.

> He will bring back many of the people of Israel to the Lord their God. And he will go on before the Lord, in the spirit and power of Elijah, to turn the hearts of the parents to their children and the disobedient to the wisdom of the righteous—to make ready a people prepared for the Lord.

When I read these verses, two words come to mind: restoration and preparation.

For starters, John would bring back many people to the Lord. On some level, this is conversion terminology. It's an expression of change. They would turn back to the one true God that they had forsaken, this having put them in the place of oppression and devastation in their time. Not only that, but John's call would affect family relationships as well— restoration would now take place between fathers (or parents) and their children. This promise hearkens back to the final words of the Old Testament found in Malachi 4. When Jews began to hear about Elijah somehow returning, they knew that redemption lay at their doorstep. Lastly, we read that wisdom would again draw the disobedient (just like in the book of Proverbs). All of this speaks of a healing and restorative act of God.

We may not have thought of this before, but according to the words of Gabriel, restoration was an essential responsibility for John: in relationship with God, with others, and the wise ways of God.

Not only that, but John was to prepare the way for the coming Messiah. Whereas the call of restorative healing reached back to the

4. Green, *The Gospel of Luke*, 75.

less-familiar message of Malachi 4, these words about preparation connected to the more well-known promises of Isaiah 40. If you take the time to read the entire chapter, the song-like poem carries quite the pull. It is one of justice, good news, and God's faithfulness and character. It ends with these memorable words:

> Do you not know?
> Have you not heard?
> The LORD is the everlasting God,
> the Creator of the ends of the earth.
> He will not grow tired or weary,
> and his understanding no one can fathom.
> He gives strength to the weary
> and increases the power of the weak.
> Even youths grow tired and weary,
> and young men stumble and fall;
> but those who hope in the LORD
> will renew their strength.
> They will soar on wings like eagles;
> they will run and not grow weary,
> they will walk and not be faint. (Isa 40:28–31)

Restoration and preparation.

These two words encapsulate much of the vocation of John the Baptizer long ago as he ushered in the first advent of Israel's Messiah. They also purposefully speak to the church's call today as we move ever closer to the final advent of Christ. We are to be a people who embody restoration in a broken world today, and we are to prepare the way for the day when "the wedding of the Lamb has come, and his bride has made herself ready" (Rev 19:7).

John answered the call back then.

It's our turn now.

CHAPTER 7: THE FORERUNNER

Questions for Reflection

1. Read over Zechariah's Spirit-filled song in Luke 1:68–79. What characteristics grab your attention most? Why might that be?

2. Considering John's ministry role in his time, one aspect we reflected on was the church's restorative role—restoring relationship with God, with others, and to the wise ways of God. What are some practical things we can do today to live this out?

3. The other facet we considered from John's life was preparation. Read over Isaiah 40 and take note of some key points that you find. What might it look like for these to also become real in our world now?

CHAPTER 8

The Announcement

When the angel Gabriel stood before Mary, the hypothetical
gave way to the real. The ordinary stories all at once glistened
under the extraordinary light of this celestial storyteller.

—RUSS RAMSEY[1]

Every day, most of us wake up with a rhythm. If yours is anything like mine, it goes something like this: Alarm goes off. We hit snooze a couple of times. Next, we roll out of bed and sluggishly limp into the bathroom, flip the switch, and squint the eyes. We undress and lift our creaking legs into the delight of a warm shower. After about ten minutes, we finish the routine by drying off, re-dressing, and applying all sorts of things that help with facial blemishes and body odor.

Now it's time to move into the kitchen for that first hot beverage of choice. Usually, my wife has already made the coffee before I appear on the scene, for which I am grateful. For most of us, we then move toward one of a few different paths—preparing some sort of nourishment for our bellies, snuggling into a favorite chair for some quiet reflection, or preparing for the little ones to emerge from their nightly slumber. After all the initial activities, the day continues forward, mirroring the previous days.

And this pattern happens just about every day.

1. Ramsey, *The Advent of the Lamb of God*, 125.

There is nothing wrong with it. It's a rhythm that makes life manageable.

Now imagine that, as you put that first cup of coffee to your lips, words ring forth from just behind you. You hear a firm yet gentle greeting. Last you knew, as you quietly exited the bedroom, your spouse was still asleep in bed. You are also aware that this voice can't be one of the kids. It is too deep and pronounced.

With all of this knowledge, you stop dead in your tracks, steady yourself, and slowly turn to peer over your shoulder. There, before you, stands a being of the most remarkable light. He holds a towering presence and his brightness floods the room in which he stands.

I imagine this is similar to the experience Mary had some two thousand years ago. Perhaps there was no ten-minute shower nor a cup of coffee. And there were no husband and kiddos nestled in the varying rooms around the home, at least none that belonged to her.

But there she was—a mid-to-late teen minding her own business, perhaps daydreaming of her upcoming wedding. And then the angel of the Lord appeared to her.

So very unsuspecting. Like the time the angel of the Lord had appeared to Moses. Moses was shepherding the flock and, voila, an angelic voice calls out from a burning bush. Mary may have been engaged in some household chore, and, without warning, Gabriel descended upon her home. His arrival was amidst her simple, daily rhythm; it came at a most unexpected time.

The first words he voices are these: "Greetings, you who are highly favored! The Lord is with you" (Luke 1:28).

What was even more shocking was the angel had appeared to a young woman of no special status. Keep this in mind for the moment.

As we peruse the four Gospel accounts in the New Testament, we will note obvious similarities among them—in the words and actions of Jesus, in the parables told, in the miracles wrought. Yet, there are definite differences to observe as well. In many ways, these narratives are like four photographers capturing the same photo, but from four distinct angles. And when it comes to the birth announcement of Jesus, we find accounts in only two of the four

Gospels. One is given to Joseph in Matthew 1:18–25 and another to Mary in Luke 1:26–38.

Both versions have essential details, but Luke's account has caught my attention here.

Why?

Luke was intent on highlighting God's work in quite an unconventional way. For starters, he was keen to stress how God moves amongst the marginalized and lowly. In the social structures of the ancient world, this included women. Particularly in Luke's Gospel, we find that God is the great reverser of fortunes, humbling the proud and lifting up the poor.

It isn't that God was opposed to giving special assignments to women, nor that the angel of the Lord had never appeared to women. We get hints of such distinct work and appearances throughout the Old Testament—Hagar, Miriam, Deborah, Samson's mother, and Huldah, to name a few. Yet, overall, we find very few occurrences recorded.

Not only did the angel appear to a woman, Mary, but he showed up at her home in Nazareth (Luke 1:26). We may already be aware that very few thought anything good could emerge from this town (see John 1:46). Furthermore, Nazareth was in the northern part of the land in Galilee. More than the town itself, the whole area of Galilee was loathed (see John 7:52). It was an area filled with more Gentiles.

A woman.

A woman from Nazareth.

A woman from Nazareth in Galilee.

Three strikes and you're out!

But God doesn't care about backgrounds—be they in regards to gender, social status, or geography. The angel of the Lord appeared to and shocked even Mary, declaring: "Greetings you who are highly favored! The Lord is with you" (Luke 1:28).

Twice Mary was told that she was *favored*—verses 28 and 30. While this term may trigger all sorts of notions of merit and earning, that is far from what the word means. At its core is the all-important Greek word *charis*. We usually translate it as *grace*. The angel had appeared, and the first words spoken are ones of grace.

Highly favored. Generously graced.

Remember, this was quite a surprise for Mary. To get a sense of the perplexity of it all, note the response: "Mary was *greatly troubled* at his words and *wondered what kind of greeting* this might be" (Luke 1:29, emphasis mine). Matthew's account tells of Joseph as the graced one to receive an appearance from the angel. But Luke flips the script. Russ Ramsey puts it this way: "It must have been strange to stand before this seraph dressed in light, strong and otherworldly, and hear him tell her not to be afraid. Perhaps it was even stranger for Mary to discover that God had formed an overall impression of her. She was known by God, and he favored her."[2]

Me, favored?, Mary must have thought.

Mary's ears caught another astonishing message from the angel: "The Lord is with you" (Luke 1:28). Joseph had been told that his son's name would be Immanuel, "God with us," a name that was to speak of God being with the entire community of God's people. But the angel here told Mary that the Lord was with *her*, personally.

Indeed, God had told his people many times that he was with them. The likes of Gideon and David (male warriors) had received these words personally. But now an angel utters them to a young virgin.

If we could only feel the genuine shock she must have felt.

Now it's time for Gabriel to step things up even more. And by more, I mean paradigm-shifting-never-gonna-happen-again-in-history more.

We are about to journey into the territory of the virgin birth.

Mary's pregnancy was not going to take place once she and her husband had consummated the marriage. Instead, it would happen through the miraculous work of the Spirit of God.

We already noted the three strikes about Mary—woman, Nazarene, Galilean. Now we have a pregnancy that does not happen in the marriage union. I can't imagine the jolt these circumstances brought. Because we have read the account so many times, it has lost its shock-value. But try and picture yourself there as a bystander,

---

2. Ramsey, *The Advent of the Lamb of God*, 125.

a fly on the wall. Imagine the expressions that would have moved across Mary's face as she listened to this heavenly being speak.

How was this all going to happen?

There is an intriguing word utilized by Luke. Many of our English translations have it as *overshadow*. It's the same root word we find in the account of Jesus's transfiguration: a bright cloud covered (*overshadowed*) those present (Matt 17:5). And Luke likewise made use of the terminology in Acts when describing the unique way in which Peter had once healed many sick people: " . . . people brought the sick into the streets and laid them on beds and mats so that at least Peter's *shadow might fall* on some of them as he passed by" (Acts 5:15, emphasis mine). Perhaps this biblical term also refers back to Genesis 1, where we read that the Spirit of God was *hovering* over the waters.[3]

Though our ability to metaphysically explain this whole phenomenon is quite limited, we can say that God's overshadowing always leaves a mark of grace. Sometimes it will catch us by surprise; at other times, it will be amid our intentional seeking of him. Even more, do not be surprised when this grace shows up amongst the most unlikely of societal outcasts. But our lives, and the lives of those around us, will experience God's generous favor as he comes near to us by the presence of his Spirit.

Moving on, we encounter the final words of Gabriel spoken to Mary: "For no word from God will ever fail" (Luke 1:37). The literal sense of this statement is this: it is *not* impossible for God's word to come to pass. We are likely aware of this truth from passages such as Matthew 19:26: "with God all things are possible."

What a comfort to Mary—and us.

We must recall to mind that we have never known the unfaithfulness of God. I am gripped regularly with my unfaithfulness. But never with God's.

For no word from God will ever fail.

---

3. Note Eugene Peterson's paraphrase translation of Luke 1:35 in *The Message*: "The Holy Spirit will come upon you, the power of the Highest *hover over* you; Therefore, the child you bring to birth will be called Holy, Son of God" (emphasis mine).

Mary was part of a vulnerable population. She came out of a despised town and region. A virgin would conceive what was inconceivable. Yet, with everything seemingly standing against her, what the angel had spoken would undoubtedly take place.

She responded: "I am the Lord's servant. May your word be fulfilled" (Luke 1:38). It was the only appropriate response. And it came from the most unlikely of persons from the most unlikely of places. Again, don't be surprised when God's gracious activity takes place amongst the least of these.

Long ago, on a day like any other day, an angel of the Lord appeared to a nobody in a land of nobodies. It set a history-altering moment in motion, one of turning the tables on the proud, powerful, and prosperous. It was one of proclaiming that the humble, hungry, and helpless would receive mercy, strength, and goodness of God.

What an announcement.

What a faithful response.

CHAPTER 8: THE ANNOUNCEMENT

Questions for Reflection

1. Have you ever listened to a unique testimony from someone who seemed to be the most improbable of people to encounter God's grace? What was their story, and what made it so difficult for you to believe it?

2. Meditate, or slowly reflect, on Mary's response to the angel: "I am the Lord's servant. May your word be fulfilled." How might these words become a prayer in your life today?

Chapter 9

At Just the Right Time

Time is a gift of God, a means of worship . . . The practice of
liturgical time teaches me, day by day, that time is not mine.
It does not revolve around me. Time revolves around God—
what he has done, what he is doing, and what he will do.

—Tish Harrison Warren[1]

I have spent quite a few years in higher education teaching on the
subject of the Old Testament. It is such a challenging task due to the
dense and exceptionally foreign nature of this portion of the Bible.
It truly is unfamiliar territory for those of us living in the twenty-
first century.

Still, truth be told, I love breaking open this part of the Bible,
both for my own life and others—from the early creation story in
Genesis to Abraham's calling and the covenant God made with him.
We are soon on to Exodus and the inspiring narrative of the deliverance of the Hebrews. This is followed by the sometimes perplexing
details of the Torah-Law that fills out the rest of the Pentateuch.
We then turn the pages to the accounts of the judges and kings,
filled with countless gruesome battles, but even more importantly,
with characters contending with the demands and questions of life.
Right smack in the middle of the Old Testament, we slow down to
take a refreshing drink from the poetry of the Psalms and Wisdom

1. Warren, *Liturgy of the Ordinary*, 108.

writings. Lastly, we enter the backdrop of the Prophets' potent words, listening in to their call for God's justice, all the while promising a future hope of restoration.

That is merely a summary of the immense and mysterious grandeur of the Hebrew Bible, what we call the Old Testament. Oh, yes, it has its challenges. And many of them, at that! Don't let anyone tell you otherwise. But I think that is part of the appeal—at least that is what I have come to believe. The questions and mystery remind us that we will not grasp these writings entirely. We will not solve all the riddles. Instead, we can revel in the knowledge that God has chosen to speak in a way that provokes *trust* over the mastering of information. Peterson says it well:

> I sometimes marvel that God chose to risk his revelation in the ambiguities of language. If he had wanted to make sure that the truth was absolutely clear, without any possibility of misunderstanding, he should have revealed his truth by means of mathematics. Mathematics is the most precise, unambiguous language that we have. But then, of course, you can't say "I love you" in algebra.[2]

Perhaps we sometimes want a text that we do not have. But this is the Bible we have, the one that God meant for us to have. And, so, I read and ask questions about Scripture with much of this in mind.

As each school year kicks off, I start back at the beginning of the Bible. With this, I get to journey afresh with the students in my Old Testament course. As we move along, there is one question I always pose for class discussion: *Why did Christ come so late?*

It's a genuine question. Why the delay?

Why not arrive in Genesis 4?

Why not prior to the Hebrew people's enslavement in Egypt?

Why not just before or just after the giving of the Torah at Mount Sinai?

Why not spare the Jews the destruction of the temple, their land, and the banishment to Babylon?

---

2. Peterson, *Eat This Book*, 93.

All of these seem like a much better moment for God to enter the world of his people. At least from my small, uninformed perspective.

Yet, we find some critical words right in the middle of Paul's letter to the Galatians:

> But when the set time had fully come, God sent his Son, born of a woman, born under the law, to redeem those under the law, that we might receive adoption to sonship. (Gal 4:4–5)

As Paul stresses, Christ came *when the set time had fully come.* There seems to have been no better period. Not a moment earlier, not a moment later.

This is still baffling. At least I think it is, if I am honest.

But here is something I have come to understand. It's something with which I am gradually, even painfully, coming to grips. God best knows *when* and *how* to act. And—while that comes across as a striking statement of trust—at times, it makes it no less difficult for me to swallow.

Please know that I have zero interest in sounding off a spiritual quip that may fit nicely on a bumper sticker. Something like, "God's when is not your when!" I am confident it would be of little help. Grappling with the when and how of God is where trust and real-life regularly meet together. It's in that tension of waiting and hoping that we previously considered. We may be the ones who muse over a theological question about why God's Messiah didn't arrive much earlier in his people's story, but the Jews had to walk that question out. It hit them over and over. They were crying aloud the words of the psalmist, "How long, LORD" (Ps 13:1)?

Still, we find ourselves asking very similar questions within our setting. We, too, have our battles with the "timing" of God.

Engulfed in despair, hanging by threads of hope, we wonder: *When will you answer us?*

Embattled by the trials of life, imagining a world that operates as God intends, we ask: *When will you come through?*

The truth is that we are heard and seen by the All-Knowing One. His eyes and ears turn toward us. I recall the words that the Lord spoke to Moses from the burning bush:

> I have indeed *seen* the misery of my people in Egypt. I have *heard* them crying out because of their slave drivers, and I am concerned about their suffering. (Ex 3:7, emphasis mine)

My heart leaps with hope as I remember them even now. Our Father is the One who sees and hears—our misery and crying—even when we may struggle to communicate it.

We have our personal inquiries into the work and timing of God. Yet, we also collectively voice a question that parallels that of the Hebrews two thousand years ago. *How long must we wait until Christ comes again?* In the Advent season, we look toward the horizon, asking God to send Christ once again to complete what he started so long ago. He sees and hears us. He really does.

But when the set time had fully come . . .

God knows *when* to act, and he knows *how* to act.

. . . God sent his Son, born of a woman, born under the law, to redeem those under the law, that we might receive adoption to sonship.

Jesus stepped into a real-world setting in his day. He did so not as an other-worldly presence that begrudgingly endured their situation. He unassumingly entered a Jewish world as a Jew—one in which he looked like a Jew, talked like a Jew, thought like a Jew, ate like a Jew. This is how God acts in our world. This is a participatory and incarnational mission.

Paul even tells us that God sent his Son "in the likeness of sinful flesh" (Rom 8:3). Jesus got down in the dirt and grime with actual humans who had a real and substantial sin problem. It's utterly astounding if you think about it. He is also with us in our brokenness. And, through Christ, we see he doesn't back away even when we have been the cause of suffering, for ourselves and others.

He sees.

He hears.

He comes.

At just the right time.

In just the right manner.

He comes.

He suffers.

He endures.

God knows when to act and he knows how to act. That is Immanuel, the God who truly is with us.

CHAPTER 9: AT JUST THE RIGHT TIME

Questions for Reflection

1. In this chapter, I have offered a statement I believe is worth pondering: *God best knows when and how to act.* While we may feel our Christian background requires us to accept that claim unequivocally, no questions asked, how easy is it to trust this?

2. What is a recent situation where you have known that God sees and hears you? What led you to believe that he was attentive to what is going on in those specific circumstances?

3. Is there someone in your life who may need to know God sees and hears them? How might you be the eyes and ears of God for them?

CHAPTER 10

The Arrival

At the heart of our Christmas spirituality is the mystery
that God of very God became man of very man to destroy
the power of evil and to restore creature and creation to
God's intention for the world. Christmas as the fulfillment
of our Advent expectation teaches that the work of restoring
creation has begun.

–ROBERT WEBBER[1]

Luke chapter 2 has to stand as one of the most read passages of
Scripture during the Advent and Christmas seasons. In it, we
discover the very early account of Jesus's birth, which included
the appearance of the angel of the Lord and the heavenly hosts to
the shepherds. When I refer to Luke's *early* account, what I mean
is that Jesus had only just been born. Matthew's report contained
an announcement (in Matt 1), as does Luke's. But Matthew then
skips forward a bit in the next chapter. Noting that the magi would
have most likely traveled from a distant eastern land, some scholars
project Jesus to have been between the ages of one and two at the
time of their arrival. However, Luke gives us an account of what
immediately took place at the time of Jesus's birth.

---

1. Webber, *Ancient-Future Time*, 61.

In the third Gospel, the angels announced three present elements at the birth of the Christ-child: joy, peace, and favor.

JOY

As the angel appeared to the shepherds, these were the first words spoken: "Do not be afraid. I bring you good news that will cause great joy for all the people" (Luke 2:10).

Of course, we catch the usual first response of the angel: "Do not be afraid." It needed to be said. As we would be, the shepherds were *terrified* (Luke 2:9). They had just experienced something they previously never had. These men *feared with great fear*, as the passage could be literally translated.

The angel quickly moves into the point of his arrival: "I bring you good news that will cause great joy for all the people." What a declaration spoken by this heavenly being! The good news was here, and the first people to have that news spoken to them were shepherds. Dirty, foul, forgotten shepherds.

The good news—the evangel—that the angel announces is this: "Today in the town of David a Savior has been born to you; he is the Messiah, the Lord" (Luke 2:11). That was the gospel of which the Jews had been agonizingly waiting for centuries. One was to come out of David's town, which meant his lineage as well, and this unique person would be Savior, Messiah, and Lord. He was to be their Deliverer from the plight of exile, sin, and death. And he would be able to accomplish this because he would be the Anointed King and Master over all. There is little doubt that these titles attributed to Jesus stand as a counter to the ruler we read about in Luke 2:1, Caesar Augustus.[2]

The Jews were finally entering the apex of God's story, and God would do all he promised he would do. He was going to do it through Jesus.

What would be the effect of this good news?

Joy.

---

2. Green, *The Gospel of Luke*, 133–34.

It was going to be great joy, which would now stand in contrast to the great fear the shepherds had initially experienced.[3]

In Greek, that word *great* comes from *megas* (think our word "mega"). It was to be a joy that surpassed all other joys! Their response would not be unlike the magi's reaction in Matthew 2:10: "When they saw the star, they were *overjoyed*" (emphasis mine).

This news was to cause great joy for all the people—for shepherds and magi, men and women, young and old, Jews and Gentiles. For all!

But what is joy?

At its root, this little word connects to another important concept—*grace*. Joy finds its foundation in grace. Upon further investigation, I think another synonym for joy would be *delight*. When we find joy in someone or something, we are delighting in that person or object. When we are delighting in someone or something, we are expressing joy at the presence of that person or object.

The good news of God awakens immeasurable joy and delight. The two go hand in hand.

Do not be afraid. I bring you good news that will cause great joy and delight for all the people.

The good news was that, in Jesus, God was sending his Deliverer, Messiah, and Lord.

PEACE

If it wasn't already frightful enough to find one angel present, Luke tells us that a "great company of the heavenly host appeared with the angel" (Luke 2:13). An army of light has come near. Spare these poor shepherds a heart attack, please, Lord!

They arrive belting forth praise:

> Glory to God in the highest heaven,
>   and on earth peace to those on whom his favor rests.
> (Luke 2:14)

---

3. Green, *The Gospel of Luke*, 133.

A short chorus of praise, if ever there was one. These words would have been sung and sung loudly. I picture the shepherds with hairs standing on their necks and arms, mouths gaping. They were so blown away by the angelic choir that they had to go and see what the angel had spoken of earlier. What was going on in the town of David? I imagine the angels expected such a response. They would show up, speak, sing, and the shepherds would go. And that's what happened. They lost no time in heading straight for Bethlehem.

In this short chorus, we observe another key word. This word is just as common as joy in the Christian community: peace.

We derive our term *irenic* from the Greek word for peace [*eirene*]. For the Hebrews, peace [*shalom*] referred to well-being and wholeness. It's a word of approval, an expression of God showing his face and smile to his people. This takes us back to the blessing the priests were to pronounce over the Israelites:

> The LORD bless you
>> and keep you;
> the LORD make his face shine on you
>> and be gracious to you;
> the LORD turn his face toward you
>> and give you peace. (Num 6:24–26)

The announcement of Christ's arrival meant tumultuous judgment for the proud, for evil rulers, and the hoarding rich (see Mary's song in 1:46–55). But this angelic chorus reiterated that God had turned his face toward the humble and broken.

Joy and delight.

Peace and well-being.

FAVOR

We find one more word in the angels' refrain that I believe is worth exploring: favor.

> Glory to God in the highest heaven,
>> and on earth peace to those on whom his favor rests.
> (Luke 2:14)

The word communicates that God's goodwill and pleasure are now resting on humanity. Still, many of us find it difficult to believe God has our good in mind. It almost seems unbiblical to say God is *pleased* with us. And keep it at a whisper's level (lest judgment fall upon us from the religious leaders).

As we've discussed, we live in a world full of hurt, pain, sin, tragedy, and disease. We find ourselves continually asking the question, *why?* We are almost agnostic at times, not quite sure if we believe what we say we know in our heads.

And it's okay. God is not scared of our questions or our doubts.

But God does have our good in mind. Because of Christ, we experience God's pleasure remaining with us. Christ is the embodiment of God. It's not just that Christ is like God, but that God is like Christ. And he is the most tangible, definitive confirmation that God has good intentions toward us.

In Christ, God was reconciling all things to himself. If that doesn't display the favor and goodwill that God has toward us, I am not sure what will. God's favor rests on us.

The words of the angel and the heavenly choir moved these shepherds. As noted, they dashed off to Bethlehem and found Mary, Joseph, and the baby. What their eyes discovered at that moment was seemingly less spectacular than the earlier angelic appearances. A very young woman and her husband were present, along with their newborn, who lay in some kind of feeding trough of all things. Yet, something struck them as they scanned the room and their eyes fell upon the baby. There was no halo around his head. Luke's report does not tell us that angels were present. The utter amazement, I think, was the shepherds' own realization that what the angels had announced was going to be true. A baby had been born, and this baby would be the Deliverer. They had heard it, but now they had seen it with their own eyes.

Perhaps these dirty men were the first evangelists. The shepherds headed out and spread the news of what they had both heard and seen, leaving others amazed as well (Luke 2:17–18). They even tried their hand at imitating the angels (Luke 2:20).

Hey, let's see if we can sing it out like the angels.
Yeah, I don't think that's going to be possible.

Okay, let's just go for it as best we can. In unison, at the top of our lungs.

Sounds good.

One, two, three . . .

They returned to the fields and their flocks (hoping the sheep were still there) with praise—maybe not to angelic levels, but probably in a way like never before.

Joy and delight.

Peace and well-being.

Favor and goodwill.

These belong to us, and we see their most significant expression in the advent of Christ.

CHAPTER 10: THE ARRIVAL

Questions for Reflection

1. In this chapter, we looked at how *great joy* was going to re-
   place the shepherd's *great fear*. Can you remember a time in
   your own life when you were overcome with great distress but
   found that, as God acted in your life, great joy and delight su-
   perseded that fear?

2. Romans 5:1–2 is one of the most well-known passages about
   the peace—or well-being and wholeness—that is ours in and
   through Jesus. Take a moment to read and reflect on Paul's
   words. What stands out from this remarkable statement from
   Paul?

3. It may be that many of us find it difficult to believe God has our
   good in mind. Perhaps we imagine he has *his* good in mind.
   But ours? It couldn't be. Take a moment and ponder what it
   might mean for God's favor and goodwill to rest upon you.
   What impressions come to mind? How might you continue to
   root yourself in the truth that God's favor rests on his people?

Chapter 11

The Untidy Story

This Child did not come into a perfect family, filled with
perfect people, who did not need saving. His birth was
scandalous . . . He came into a messed-up, imperfect family
like yours and mine. He came to save us from our sins, to set
God's world right again, and to dwell with us . . .

–Tom Fuerst[1]

There's a small problem that can be present within the church as we
head into the Advent and Christmas seasons. In this case, I do not
speak of being enamored with consumerism. I previously walked
through the challenge of the "mall religion" of our day, so I need not
rehash that. The problem I am referring to now is how the church
can couch the Advent and Christmas stories within an overly perfect and pristine setting.

What we may easily forget is that the actual storyline in the
Bible is not as tidy as first thought. Sure, the newborn Christ in an
animal feeding-trough could be considered unhygienic. We could
talk about the phrases "silent night" and "all is calm"—how they
may fail to encapsulate the real situation at hand, that no childbirth
is quiet and orderly. Anyone who has been present at the birth of a
child can attest to this. Not to mention Jesus was an actual human

1. Fuerst, *Underdogs and Outsiders*, 90.

baby, complete with all the noises, smells, bodily activities, and needs of a newborn. The imagination runs wild when picturing the tangibly untidy situation into which this new king was born.

However, what I have described pales in comparison with the broader framework we find in the Gospel accounts.

As we saw earlier, Christ's story doesn't begin in Matthew 1:18. According to the Gospel writer, and the ancient custom of recounting a person's life, the account should start with Matthew 1:1. The hard-to-pronounce, and not so hard-to-pronounce, names remind modern folk like you and I that we are entering a centuries-long storyline that led up to the birth of the Messiah.

But what of all these names? Some of them seem more worthy of recognition—perhaps Abraham, Boaz, David, and Solomon. Others, not so much. Still, each of the four men just mentioned has his own complications. Some of those will become clearer in a moment. However, if we are honest, four other names make the account even more difficult to swallow.

Tamar.

Rahab.

Ruth.

Bathsheba.[2]

In the ancient world, these names could have been considered a great blight upon the lineage of the one called God's Messiah. I don't think we can feel the strain that would have been present for some Jews as they heard or read Matthew's recounting of the family lineage of Jesus. Moreover, knowing the backgrounds of these women, if they were to walk into one of our Sunday services today, they undoubtedly would receive tense-filled glares from many. Someone might even ask them to leave.

We find Tamar's story in Genesis 38. It's not as familiar, probably having never been covered in Sunday School or in a Sunday sermon. With that, you may want to take a moment and read through it. You will very soon understand that this story is not rated PG. To sum up, the repugnant Canaanite, Tamar, got pregnant through her father-in-law, Judah. She apparently had dressed

---

2. Bathsheba is called "Uriah's wife" (Matt 1:6).

like a prostitute—or at least her attire made it seem as if she was a prostitute. And Judah needed a "favor." Remember, men were the ones who ruled in an ancient, patriarchal society.

Later on, following their encounter, Tamar is exposed. Of course, it is much easier to catch women. Their ever-expanding belly gives them away. If the man goes unseen, he can move about incognito—and there would be no DNA test back then to confirm the father. With this, Tamar becomes a public disgrace to the family name and, thus, Judah wants her burned to death. Were it not for Tamar's quick wits, he would have got away with it. But she had held on to Judah's treasured possessions—his seal, cord, and staff. Still, as the birth of your twins drew near, how awkward would it be to explain that the father of your children was your father-in-law? Doubtful, this story would make it to the testimony microphone on a Sunday. Nonetheless, even with what may be considered Tamar's sketchy choices, Judah was pressed into the accurate declaration: "She is more righteous than I . . . " (Gen 38:26).

Tamar in the line of the Messiah.

Shameful.

If we are uncertain of Tamar's prostitution, the Bible clearly labels Rahab as such (see Josh 2:1; Heb 11:31). Really?! A pagan woman from the red-light district makes it into Jesus's family line. Allow the dust to settle for a moment on that one.

Rahab indeed helped the Hebrew people, though only through a bit of deception (Josh 1:4–7). Knowing the hand of the Lord was on the Hebrews, she worked her magic to enter into a deal of safe harbor with the spies. She knew what every Israelite was to confess: "the LORD your God is God in heaven above and on the earth below" (Josh 2:11). Her name has even been inserted in the proverbial "Hall of Faith" in Hebrews 11.

A prostitute and liar has made it into the line of the Messiah. It is interesting to note that Jesus went out of his way to eat meals with prostitutes during his public ministry. Perhaps some of this was fueled by his own family story.

Rahab in the line of the Messiah.

Disgraceful.

Of the four women mentioned in Jesus's lineage, Ruth seems the least problematic. In our day, we recognize her as a heroine of the Bible. Many may also view the biblical book after her name as a manual for Christian dating—which it isn't. Yet, while we have a thoroughly optimistic view of Ruth thousands of years later, we cannot forget the tension that permeates the text. Her story is worth exploring further.

By the time of its writing, the Israelites would have extinguished most of the Canaanites from the land. If you recall, both Tamar and Rahab had a Canaanite background. But Ruth, she was a Moabite. This was a group of people living *outside* of the land. A truly heathen and idolatrous people! Not only that, but the Moabites had come from an incestuous relationship between Lot and his daughters (see Gen 19:30–38). As Tom Fuerst summarizes in his Advent study, "In short, in Israel's imagination all Moabites fall under the moniker of incestuous, inhospitable, idolatrous foreigners."[3]

Ruth is part of this people.

Moreover, as it came time to instruct Ruth about how she might save the family and their inheritance, Naomi offered some questionable advice, at least by our reckoning. This is further confirmed by Ruth's actions, though our English translations don't clearly reveal this (see Ruth 3:7). The expression "good spirits," referencing Boaz's condition following his evening feast, shows a man who had had his fill of fermented drink. Furthermore, the phrases "uncovered his feet" and "lay down" insinuate a rather dubious rendezvous. Boaz was drunk, and this was, on some level, a sexual encounter.[4] Again, this is not a Christian dating manual.

Ruth in the line of the Messiah.

Appalling.

It is of some interest to consider why Matthew leaves Bathsheba nameless. I imagine this is because the emphasis was on David and Solomon. Still, he is very intentional to slide in the reference "Uriah's wife." He wants to remind us of Solomon's origin and background.

3. Fuerst, *Underdogs and Outsiders*, 50.
4. Fuerst, *Underdogs and Outsiders*, 54–55.

But before all of that, Bathsheba was married to Uriah. We are not entirely sure of Bathsheba's ancestry. Her father Eliam was likely the same Eliam in David's "thirty" (2 Sam 11:3; 2 Sam 23:34). The Bible tells us Eliam was the son of Ahithophel, who was a Gilonite. The Gilonites hailed from Judah. Noting the backstory, this means that Bathsheba was likely an Israelite. But because of her marriage to Uriah, of Hittite descent, she would have been easily viewed as a non-Israelite.[5]

Bathsheba was not to fault for the circumstances in which she found herself. Modern-day purity culture must never claim that she should have been more modest in her bathing choices. It was completely acceptable for a woman to wash outside the home, especially when purifying herself from her monthly cycle (2 Sam 11:4). This background brings greater awareness as to why she would have been outside under the veil of nightfall. But king David, the one labeled as a "man after God's own heart," took Bathsheba for a "night out."

He followed up the incident by assigning her husband to a place of certain death while in battle—"out in front where the fighting is fiercest" (2 Sam 11:15). Bathsheba was now left to marry the man who had violated her. She would soon bear the child, and that child would die just a week after its birth. What a truly grievous account! Solomon would be concieved in this scandalous union between David and Bathsheba (2 Sam 12:24). A storyline of betrayal, adultery, and murder.

Bathsheba in the line of the Messiah.

Unspeakable.

That was the larger backstory to Jesus's birth.

What about the immediate period leading up to Christ's birth?

We have already taken a look at the angel's announcement to Mary, as seen through Luke's Gospel. I noted that she was a woman from Nazareth in Galilee, a despised place. A young woman, perhaps in her mid-teens, has now become mysteriously pregnant. Think of Joseph, his family, and his extended family. Imagine Mary's immediate and extended family. Add on top of that the synagogue community and wider cultural setting. Yet, we still accept her story

5. France, *The Gospel of Matthew*, 36–37.

as a sweet and untarnished part of the Messiah's family line. But this was no simple situation.

Up to this point, everything just recounted takes place before we even move out of Matthew chapter 1!

The next chapter tells of visitors from the east who have come to worship the newborn king of the Jews. While the word *magi* can't be defined with absolute precision, this group probably had some connection to astrology and even the magical arts. Hence, it was not the Scriptures that drew them to Jerusalem, but rather a star in the heavens. Hence, why we think they were astrologers of some sort. They were the ones asking where they could find this new king.

Of further significance is that the chief priests and teachers of the law knew exactly where the Messiah was to be born, presumably because they had been the ones studying the Bible. They are quick to answer Herod's query with the words from the prophet Micah. You'd think that they would have been ready for Jesus's birth. But they weren't. Instead, it's some eastern astrologers who sought him out. The Jewish leaders knew the Scriptures, but it meant nothing to them.

Matthew's account of Jesus's birth ends with the family fleeing to Egypt and then finally settling back into the town of Nazareth. We've already considered Nazareth, but let us not forget what a Jewish response would have been upon hearing of Egypt. The Jews knew their Bible stories and history. Egypt was the oppressive, pagan enemy from long ago.

In all, what we have here is the not-so-tidy Christmas story. There is just no other way to slice it. This is the disgraced birth account of Jesus, God's Messiah. In many ways, our carols have missed some of the critical details. I am not sure our Christmas pageants do any better.

In reflecting upon all of this, I realize that God continually chooses to do great works of grace through the non-elite, the despised, the hated, and the outcasts. Paul tells us that it is the cross of Christ that displays God's power and wisdom (see 1 Cor 1:18–31). God always seems to do things in contrast to what we—both the world and the church—imagine as good and right.

It's not that God turns from those who have possessions and are well-liked. But we must recognize *why* he has provided so much in our lives. It is so that we might extend the generous grace of God to others—the impoverished, despised, and forgotten. That's why he first chose Abraham long ago. That was Israel's charge as well.

We must recall in this season of Advent and Christmas that God is ready to perform beautiful, restorative acts of grace amongst the broken and oppressed, the sick and the poor. He looks for a people prepared to embark on such a mission with him, one that draws close to and invites the Tamar's and Rahab's, the Ruth's and Bathsheba's, the mysteriously pregnant, and the magi astrologers.

That is what we discover with Christ's birth. He was the one who came not to be served but to serve and give his life a ransom. Matthew will be sure to remind us of this later on (Matt 20:25–28).

This is the untidy Christmas story we are to tell.

This is the untidy Christmas story we are to live.

CHAPTER 11: THE UNTIDY STORY

Questions for Reflection

1. Which story about the four women listed in Matthew's genealogy struck you most? Consider further study of the specific
   account of that woman, as told in the Old Testament.

2. Spend some time reflecting on how Jesus's own life story—
   beginning with his lineage and birth—is filled with a myriad
   of people whom even religious folk despised. Those include
   the blind and diseased, to prostitutes and tax collectors, to
   the shameful and unimportant. During this season of Advent
   and Christmas, how might God utilize you in displaying acts
   of compassion and kindness to these people whom he truly
   values?

CHAPTER 12

The Ordinary Good News

*One great idea of the biblical revelation is that God is
manifest in the ordinary, in the actual, in the daily, in the now,
in the concrete incarnations of life.*

–RICHARD ROHR[1]

As we open those beginning pages of Matthew's and Luke's Gospels, we find some truly extraordinary accounts embedded within the narratives: angels announcing salvation, revelatory visions and dreams, prophetic songs, mouths struck silent, and more. The announcement and birth of Christ are no regular moments in history!

Still, while we discover the remarkable on each page, I am also struck by something quite the opposite. God's redemptive work is found within the ordinary, those daily "incarnations of life," as Richard Rohr calls them. As we read those early chapters of the Gospels, we notice God at work in the everyday moments of life, the nitty-gritty particulars of the story.

Zechariah is getting on with his priestly duty.

Mary is visiting her relative, Elizabeth.

Caesar orders a census throughout the Roman empire.

Joseph and Mary are preparing for marriage.

In a way, these are part of the ordinary rhythms and cycles of life. No one would bat an eye at these details. Of course, we

1. Rohr, *Things Hidden*, 16.

know the full story, where it's all headed. So, it's easy to gloss over these points. Yet, if we are careful enough, something might catch our eye. As with the characters in the Gospel accounts, these mundane moments represent life for us as well.

We take the bus or drive to work, arriving just in time, or perhaps late. We then hurriedly shuffle across the parking lot as shirts are freshly tucked into pants or creases are once again flattened on blouses. We make coffee, turn on our computers, and allow our bodies to drop back in our desk chairs. Our email inbox then floods forth with more information and requests from colleagues. All of this, and it's only half-past eight in the morning.

Zechariah took up his priestly position, faithful to serve even in the small. We take up our post at the office, checking email, budgeting numbers, and the like.

How long has it been since we last visited the cousins? It was during summer vacation three years ago. We packed the van from floor to ceiling, even though we were visiting for only a few days. After enduring the six-hour drive, we arrived at the door famished. Greetings ensued, filled with hugs and handshakes.

Mary traveled to visit her expectant relative, Elizabeth. We pack up our luggage and head out on a trip to see family we haven't seen in some time.

The television is turned on only to announce another press conference given by politicians. This one is about a growing frustration in international relations. Tax season has arrived, and it's time to gather the numerous documents to file by the deadline. It's been ten years since the last one, so census information now floods each family's mailbox.

Rome wanted to flex its muscle and do so by counting heads. Our governments govern to wield the power they hold.

It was only just a few weeks ago that a twenty-something young man took his beloved girlfriend on a walk by the riverfront. At one point along the path, he stops and begins the descent to one knee. He nervously shoves his hand into his pocket and pulls from its depths a small, black, velvety box. Upon opening, the young girl's eyes light up at the sparkle of the ring's encased stone. *"Will you marry me?"* the well-rehearsed words come. As tears form in her eyes, she responds with the only word she can: *"Yes!"* The couple embrace, caught up in the joyous moment of love.

Joseph and Mary awaited the day when the two shall become one. A young couple, fresh out of college, has now begun preparations for their life together.

We know these scenarios are part of our everyday lives. They accurately describe much of the day-to-day, the mundane, the routine. But that's where God frequently chooses to show up. Of course, God shows up in our community worship gatherings and prayer meetings (i.e., Acts 1:14; 13:1–3). Let us not forget this. But I think the challenge is to remember that God enters into the unassuming matters and spaces of life—in our homes and workplaces, in our neighborhoods and parks, in our restaurants and bookstores.

That's the witness of the Gospel accounts.

It's the affirmation of Scripture.

Even the testimony of history.

In her reflections on the ordinary nature of making our beds, author Tish Harrison Warren notes, "The crucible of our formation is in the monotony of our daily routines."[2] A bit further on, she continues, "I often want to skip the boring, daily stuff to get the thrill of an edgy faith. But it's in the dailiness of the Christian faith . . . that God's transformation takes root and grows."[3] Warren has hit on something vital for the Christian to understand. God is at work in our waking, the making of our beds, the brushing of our teeth, the eating of leftovers, and all the other stuff that makes up life. Every single bit of it.

Of course, most of us already hold to a theology that says God works in those ordinary places and small spaces. Yet, that theology may not have entirely moved to a "lived theology," as Eugene Peterson calls it.[4] We carry some kind of cognitive dissonance wherein we "know" something in our heads, but making it a life experience is a challenge. Peterson remarks, "There comes a time for most of

---

2. Warren, *Liturgy of the Ordinary*, 34.

3. Warren, *Liturgy of the Ordinary*, 35–36.

4 Peterson, *Christ Plays in Ten Thousand Places*, 5.

us when we discover a deep desire within us to live from the heart what we already know in our heads and do with our hands."[5]

The Advent and Christmas stories remind us that God is alive and well within the details of our lives. At times, it may knock us back: God unmistakably speaks; we burst forth in a moment of fantastic worship; we even lay hands on the sick and see them healed. Perhaps an angel also arrives in our presence. Maybe, maybe not.

Yet, think about it. Those extraordinary moments tended to arrive within the framework of the ordinary. Remember the Gospels. Zechariah was to perform the meager task of burning incense. Mary had traveled to visit a beloved relative. Rome had decided it was time for a census. Joseph and Mary had gone about their daily lives as they awaited their union.

What made those moments so extraordinary? That's just it: they weren't. But God drew near anyway.

At times, God's presence will remain somewhat veiled. A friend will arrive; they will offer a smile and extend a word of encouragement. An email from your boss shows up in your inbox, letting you know they've seen your willingness to work extra hours on the current project. Thus, they grant you the gift of a three-day weekend.

The God who arrives in the angel of the Lord also appears in the quiet cover of the sunrise. The God who painted the cosmos with billions of stars also knows the hairs on each head. God discloses himself as we work, as we cook, as we play, as we parent.

People still head to their jobs.

We continue to visit our families.

Politicians carry on making decisions.

Engaged couples continue to prepare for their great day.

Perhaps we will glimpse the work of God in those small and mundane spaces. That's the ordinary good news.

May we have eyes to see it in this season.

5. Peterson, *Christ Plays in Ten Thousand Places*, 4.

CHAPTER 12: THE ORDINARY GOOD NEWS

Questions for Reflection

1. Many times, the spectacular and the remarkable catch our attention. We want God to reveal himself in those extraordinary ways. Of course, this is not wrong. And, at times, God indeed reveals himself in such a manner. But why do you think there may be a fascination with the extraordinary? Why might it be easy to disdain the ordinary?

2. In the past, what are some of the simple and common ways that God has revealed himself to you? In particular, during Advent and Christmas, how might God be working in the ordinary moments of this season to show himself?

CHAPTER 13

Logos Become Flesh

God created our souls to be satisfied only with the divine
everlastingness of the Word made flesh.

−A.W. Tozer[1]

"In the beginning . . . " These words are familiar to most Bible
readers today. And, if one stopped with just that phrase, it may be
unclear as to whether the reference was for Genesis 1 or John 1.
But as John's audience read—or heard—those opening words to his
Prologue, they would have been transported in their minds back to
the beginning. No doubt, that was John's intent.

An even more significant point worth noting is that Genesis was not the name given by the Hebrews to the first book of
their Bible. Rather, it was the Hebrew for, you guessed it, "In the
beginning."

"In the beginning . . . "

As I remarked back in chapter one of this book, every story
begins with "once upon a time." The Bible opens this way as well. By
this, I do not mean that Scripture is false. It's simply our modern-
day expression given to summon our imaginations. When I hear
that phrase, I prepare myself to encounter some epic tale, one in the
vein of J.R.R. Tolkien or C.S. Lewis.

"Once upon a time . . . "

1. Tozer, *And He Dwelt Among Us*, 28.

"In the beginning . . . "

Turning back to Genesis, we remember that this is our beginning. Not God's, but ours. In those first few sentences, we read of a formless and empty earth, darkness present upon the deep, and a gentle brooding of the Spirit of God. These features should stick in our minds as we also encounter John's opening words. Just as it was at the start of God's unfolding creation, so it was with the arrival of the Word, Jesus.

Formless and empty.

Darkness over the deep.

God's Spirit was preparing.

In Genesis 1, God spoke, "Let there be light," and there was light. Life and light began to unfold in the songlike description of the creation. In John 1, God spoke with the arrival of his Word. Life and light sprang forth as the eternal Word appeared on the scene. With the first beginning, God saw that the light was good and separated that light from the darkness. In this new beginning, the light of God's Word would shine forth, and the darkness would not overtake it.

With this, we can see the arrival of the Word, God's Son, as the announcement of a new beginning and a new creation for God's people.

John's words in verse 14 ring of another fascinating truth of what it meant for the Word to step into our space: "The Word became *flesh* and made his dwelling among us" (emphasis mine). The theological term *incarnation* sums up these words of John. Tozer describes John's statement in this way: " . . . the apostle states the most profound mystery of human thought—how deity could cross the gulf separating what is God from what is not God."[2]

John's account can come across as the more abstract and spiritual version of the four Gospels. And it is different from what we call the Synoptics—Matthew, Mark, and Luke. Yet, John 1:14 makes it clear upfront that his account is an embodied, fleshy, and earthy account.

2. Tozer, *And He Dwelt Among Us*, 77–78.

We may have heard of the Greek used here for Word [*Logos*]. We could also translate this term as *message* or *speech*. Of course, Logos usually refers to more than just *one word*. Hence, why we consider other ways to define the Greek. As difficult as it can be to define this Greek term, at its foundation, I think this is what John was getting at: *If one looks at Jesus of Nazareth, you are truly seeing the embodied message of God.*

When Jesus spoke or acted, God himself was speaking and acting—not mere information about God, but the eternal and divine as an embodied person with flesh.[3]

Incarnation: the eternal, divine Word as flesh. It is still a challenge to fathom; it remains a challenge to explain. Walter Brueggemann declares, "It was a scandal that would, in the wisdom of the church, be made into a mystery."[4] To proclaim something as a mystery does not mean one is avoiding objective truth. But it does recognize that we are dealing with something uniquely other and holy.

"The Word became flesh and made his dwelling among us."

The term used for *dwelling* is a reference to the tent, or tabernacle, of God. You can see how John's words keep hearkening back to the Old Testament. Jewish readers would have been reminded of the gift of God's presence as known and experienced within the holy tent. Encased in this distinct center of worship was the Ark of the Covenant. And, though the tabernacle remained for some time after God's people entered Canaan, it would have been more strongly connected to Israel's period of wilderness wanderings. Life in the promised land would have reminded the people of the temple, constructed under Solomon's guidance.

The tabernacle signified God's presence drawing close amidst the hardships of wilderness wanderings. The Word becoming flesh was God's presence coming near during the traumatic wilderness under Rome's rule.

John continues in verse 14: "We have seen his glory, the glory of the one and only Son, who came from the Father, full of grace and truth."

---

3. Morris, *The Gospel According to John*, 66–67.

4. Brueggemann, *Celebrating Abundance*, 81.

Full of grace and truth. I recall a pastor friend of mine once talking about how the church's failures have led to the loss of meaning for particular words such as *church*. It has been destroyed in the mind of the world, and for many believers as well. However, he noted one word that has remained intact through it all. *Grace*. It can still be spoken, even by Christians, without disdain and disgust. This pastor friend is one who has always exemplified grace in my mind. It is no wonder the name of his church is Grace Community Church.

Christians repeatedly speak of grace, but at times it's a difficult term to nail down. In short, the grace of God is the favor of God. It is God's free and generous giving of himself to others. Yes, there are blessings given—grace gifts, if you will. But, more than that, grace is a word that encapsulates God's giving of himself. And this is what we find most uniquely in the incarnation of the Word. In Christ, we find Immanuel, God giving himself to be with us.

Don't forget that God also partners grace with truth. Truth is not some rigid, stagnant dogma by which we control the masses. Grace and truth are in relationship together. And Jesus was the direct embodiment of God's message, one full of grace and truth.

We need to pause to remember that this is who God is.

After a momentary sidetrack about John the Baptizer, the Gospel writer, John, tells us further in verse 16: "Out of his fullness we have all received grace in place of grace already given." The NIV has done well to translate the more dynamic meaning of the Greek expression "grace for grace." This phrase—"grace in the place of grace already given"—beautifully articulates the fullness of God's message that we encounter in Christ.

Back in 2003–2006, I lived in Swansea, Wales. The college where I worked was particularly close to the Swansea Bay. One day, as I was pondering this passage in John's Gospel, I was reminded of the movement of the sea's waves. As one watches them, you'll notice a consistent, rhythmic flow. Just as one wave pushes up on the shore, another follows right after it. And then another wave, which, in turn, is followed by another. It has been that way ever since God created the seas and their shores. It will continue to do so into the far future—even if we are unaware, even when we are gone.

As I was meditating on that verse and the cadenced movement of the waves, I sensed God say, "That is how my grace works."

As soon as one wave of grace arrives, before even having time to drink of that wave fully, another wave appears just behind it. And then another is followed by another. As with the seas, so it is in Christ. We experience the perpetual flow of God's free grace.

John offers something to stir the pot amongst hard-hearted Jews. In verse 17, we read, "For the law was given through Moses; grace and truth came through Jesus Christ."

At first glance, no ounce of grace seems offered through Moses and the Law-Torah. But that is inaccurate, I think. Just as the old covenant revealed truth, so the Jews could discover grace in the words of the Law-Torah. What we have here in John's Gospel is a comparison between the two great figureheads of Moses and the Word, Jesus. One now reigns supreme over the other. That's how God had always designed it.

"In the beginning . . ."

Among a formless and empty world, with darkness having settled over the deep, God's Spirit was preparing for a new beginning and a new creation. Jesus, God's great message, had become flesh. God was setting up his holy tent in their midst. The great embodiment of God's grace and truth had now taken up residence in the neighborhood.

Immanuel was here.

CHAPTER 13: LOGOS BECOME FLESH

Questions for Reflection

1. "In the beginning" was a phrase that would immediately turn the attention of the reader to Genesis 1. Consider reading both John 1:1–18 and Genesis 1. Try and note some of the parallels you see existing between the two passages but were not covered in this chapter.

2. We considered how the incarnation is genuinely part of the mystery of the Christian faith. What do you think about the aspect of mystery? Do you believe it is reasonable not to be able to explain all details of our faith?

3. Jesus is the Word—the real, embodied message of God. How might this impact the way you live and tell the message of God's good news in Christ?

4. Take a moment to further reflect on that phrase, "grace in the place of grace already given." Go back and meditate on the words found in John 1:14, 16–17. What other insights did you gain from these verses?

CHAPTER 14

Hymn of Humility

No one born of flesh will ever be greater than he. But Jesus laid
down his divine power and greatness and appeared on earth as
we all do... The mind boggles at the depth of Christ's descent.

—ADELE CALHOUN[1]

When you have walked the life Paul has, and then sit down to put
pen to paper, there is no doubt you will communicate some of the
most perceptive insights of anyone who has ever lived. Turning to a
letter like the one written to the Philippian church, I think we find
one of his more pastoral letters, written as he sat under house arrest
near the end of his life.

Paul remembered the people frequently in prayer. He is grate-
ful for their genuine partnership in the good news and he remarks:
"God can testify how I long for all of you with the affection of Christ
Jesus" (see Phil 1:3–8).

Paul was an apostle, true. But he was just as much a pastor.

When we come to chapter 2 of his letter—not just the glorious
hymn about Christ, as found in verses 6–11, but the entire section—
we get a sense of the pastoral burden of his words. He is trying to
communicate to this church, one he longs for with the affection of
Christ, what it means to walk together in grace, humility, and service.
He gets things rolling with some sincere yet pointed instruction:

1. Calhoun, *Spiritual Disciplines Handbook*, 216.

> Therefore if you have any encouragement from being
> united with Christ, if any comfort from his love, if any
> common sharing in the Spirit, if any tenderness and
> compassion, then make my joy complete by being like-
> minded, having the same love, being one in spirit and
> of one mind. Do nothing out of selfish ambition or vain
> conceit. Rather, in humility value others above your-
> selves, not looking to your own interests but each of you
> to the interests of the others. (Phil 2:1–4)

Following this little exhortation, Paul takes a diversion. He doesn't
go off-topic; instead, he brings home his point in the most appropriate way possible. His next words will become one of the most
pastorally and Christologically infused passages in all of the Bible.

To best instruct them on how to walk out the life of humility
that he is calling them to, Paul reminds them of Jesus. He does so
in songlike fashion. In calling them to prize others over self, Paul
crafts what could be called the "Hymn of Humility." His appeal to
them is that they adopt the mindset of Christ. These are his words:

> Who, being in very nature God,
>> did not consider equality with God something to be used
>> to his own advantage;
> rather, he made himself nothing
>> by taking the very nature of a servant,
>> being made in human likeness.
> And being found in appearance as a man,
>> he humbled himself
>> by becoming obedient to death—
>> even death on a cross!
> Therefore God exalted him to the highest place
>> and gave him the name that is above every name,
> that at the name of Jesus every knee should bow,
>> in heaven and on earth and under the earth,
> and every tongue acknowledge that Jesus Christ is Lord,
>> to the glory of God the Father. (Phil 2:6–11)

Here is Jesus, the one who had existed in the form of God. Divinity
was his; he was on equal footing with God. Yet, with this, we find

one of the most formidable and moving truths of the entire Christian faith: Christ made himself nothing.

Just chew on that for a moment.

Christ made himself nothing.

I know it may be easy to rush ahead to the statements about his crucifixion, or even to his exaltation and enthronement over all things. Those are key as well. But when it comes to reflecting on these words during the seasons of Advent and Christmas, I believe we need to stop with verses 6–7.

The divine Son emptied himself of his rights, laid aside any claims to those rights, and made himself nothing. This emptying of self wasn't a mere abstract idea with no foundation in real human history. It looked like something—Christ becoming a servant, being made in human likeness.

What do you do with truth this compelling?

All one can do is acknowledge the breathtakingly beautiful truth and then turn toward Christ in worship.

Again, the cross—remarkable.

Christ's resurrection—extraordinary.

His royal exaltation and reign—amazing.

But I think we need first to process the divine becoming human, God coming to us in Christ, as Immanuel. At least, as best we can. Pondering once again the accounts of Mary and Joseph, the shepherds, and the magi may help us consider our own proper response to this truth. Their eyes stared at divinity wrapped in humanity. Their hands touched God in human likeness.

God, in Christ, had moved into what Henri Nouwen called "downward mobility." In his work *Here and Now*, following a few reminders of Christ's teaching on humility and service, Nouwen remarks, "This is the way of downward mobility, the descending way of Jesus. It is the way toward the poor, the suffering, the marginal, the prisoners, the refugees, the lonely, the hungry, the dying, the tortured, the homeless—toward all who ask for compassion."[2] This way of being is very different from the life of "success, popularity, or

---

2. Nouwen, *Here and Now*, 139.

power," as Nouwen terms it. This kind of life may be very different from what we even see in the church.

Every bit of Christ's solidarity with the poor and oppressed—his "downward mobility"—flows out of his emptying of himself and becoming human like us. It is what fueled and ignited his touching of the leper, his eating with prostitutes and tax collectors, his feeding of the hungry, his embracing of the outcast. He was the servant of servants, embodying the role that was spoken of in the ancient Servant Songs (Isa 42:1–4; 49:1–6; 50:4–7; 52:13–53:12). Remember, it was his mother's song that described the true work of Jesus—he would lift the humble and fill the hungry with good things (Luke 1:46–55). Christ came not to be served, but to serve and give his life a ransom (Matt 20:25–28).

As Paul sat under the watchful eye of a Roman guard, he prepared himself to pastorally guide and instruct a people who were dear to his heart. While offering words on the noble virtues of unity and humility, in a moment of divine inspiration, Paul turned to the only source and example that would do.

Christ Jesus.

As he penned this hymn, perhaps all the while singing its tune (maybe to the displeasure of the Roman guard present), Paul captured the beauty and mystery of the incarnation. He did it like never before, and perhaps ever since.

Indeed, the "downward mobility" of Christ would eventually lead to an upward progression. But that was beside the point. Paul was teaching the Philippian community what humble service sincerely looked like. The exaltation of God's people will come. It surely would one day. But it starts in the same way that it did for Christ—emptying, laying aside, considering ourselves as nothing.

> Who, being in very nature God,
>> did not consider equality with God something to be used
>> to his own advantage;
> rather, he made himself nothing
>> by taking the very nature of a servant,
>> being made in human likeness. (Phil 2:6–7)

These words encapsulate the divine Christ, whom we follow.

CHAPTER 14: HYMN OF HUMILITY

Questions for Reflection

1. Consider the phrase in Philippians 2:7: "he made himself nothing." The Greek refers to Christ *emptying* himself. As you think of the Gospel accounts, what are some of the tangible ways we see Christ embodying a life of emptying?

2. In a world full of kings and queens back then, with presidents and prime ministers now, the words of Philippians 2:6–7 describe something thoroughly counter-cultural. Why is the way of "downward mobility" so despised in our world?

3. As noted in this chapter, the words of the "Hymn of Humility" speak into Paul's instruction to the church (see Phil 2:1–5). How can you exemplify Christlike humility to others during this time of Advent and Christmas?

Conclusion

Reflections of Immanuel

> I heard a voice thunder from the Throne: "Look! Look! God
> has moved into the neighborhood, making his home with
> men and women! They're his people, he's their God. He'll wipe
> every tear from their eyes. Death is gone for good—tears gone,
> crying gone, pain gone—all the first order of things gone."
> The Enthroned continued, "Look! I'm making everything new.
> Write it all down—each word dependable and accurate."
>
> John, the apostle (Rev 21:3–5 MSG)

Immanuel. God with us.

These words will, undoubtedly, be found on our lips during these special seasons in the church calendar. They are one of the most appropriate responses in our worship. We freshly encounter them each Advent and Christmas.

Early on, we considered the original Immanuel of Isaiah and king Ahaz's day. Though the king desired not to ask the Lord for a sign, the prophet assured him one would come anyway: "The virgin will conceive and give birth to a son, and will call him Immanuel" (Isa 7:14). If you'll recall, in the prophet's day, Immanuel most likely referred to the son we read about in Isaiah chapter 8: Maher-Shalal-Hash-Baz (see verses 1–10).

As we already know, this was also the designation given to the divine Son, the Word who became flesh. Immanuel—God would be with his people.

Neither Maher-Shalal-Hash-Baz, nor Jesus, were called by the name Immanuel. It was a prophetic marker, a kind of signpost name that characterized the promise of God in Isaiah's time, and that much more through Christ centuries later.

Though the name shows up all of three times in Scripture, twice in the Old Testament and once in the New Testament, the prophetic promise of Immanuel rings throughout all time.

Think about it for a moment.

Even after the alienation of disobedience in Genesis 3, God shows up walking in the garden in the cool—or wind—of the day (Gen 3:8). The generous grace of God was available even as failure stood nearby. God also drew close and made garments to cover their nakedness (Gen 3:21).

Immanuel, God with us.

There is the angel of the Lord who shows up numerous times throughout the Old Testament. This special messenger comes on behalf of, speaks on behalf of, and sometimes seems to be God himself. Or what of the pillar of cloud by day and the pillar of fire by night? Both were representing God's closeness as he led the Israelites throughout the wilderness wanderings.

Two of the most significant Immanuel occurrences in all of the Old Testament were the tabernacle and temple. The Hebrews were to walk into these sacred spaces and a sense of God's awesome and unfathomable presence would immediately hit them. In particular, the Hebrews most hallowed space housed the Ark of the Covenant. The hand-crafted cherubim sat on top of the Ark's cover, with God's glory choosing to rest between the two angelic figures.

God's wisdom is personified in Proverbs. The prophets' voices rang out the word of God.

Immanuel, even in the most ancient of times.

We finally turn to the New Testament, to the birth of Christ. This is the quintessential place where we remember Immanuel. But let us not forget "God with us" in the Holy Spirit who both dwells in us (John 14:17) and seals us for our future redemption (Eph 1:13–14). Not only that, but the Spirit is the one who even now empowers God's people to serve him in faithful mission. This is the story that the book of Acts tells us. Likewise, what of the body of

Christ? We are called to be Christ to one another. In a sense, we get to both be and receive God's Immanuel presence through the Spirit.

God is truly with us.

Finally, we come to Revelation 21, the very end of God's unfolding story in history. God's full and final Immanuel nature is described with beauty and grace:

> Then I saw "a new heaven and a new earth," for the first heaven and the first earth had passed away, and there was no longer any sea. I saw the Holy City, the new Jerusalem, coming down out of heaven from God, prepared as a bride beautifully dressed for her husband. And I heard a loud voice from the throne saying, "Look! God's dwelling place is now among the people, and he will dwell with them. They will be his people, and God himself will be with them and be their God. He will wipe every tear from their eyes. There will be no more death or mourning or crying or pain, for the old order of things has passed away."
>
> He who was seated on the throne said, "I am making everything new!" Then he said, "Write this down, for these words are trustworthy and true." (Rev 21:1–5)

When we pick up Scripture, turn its pages, and encounter the text through the work of the Spirit, we are left with one conclusion—God is truly with his people. He is Immanuel.

Though we particularly remember his Immanuel character in the seasons of Advent and Christmas, and such is right, we must not forget the rest of the story. Our God has shown this from the beginning and he will continue to do so even into the renewed heavens and earth.

I suppose that if we were to record all the stories of God being with us, the whole world would be filled with those volumes.[1]

These are all biblical and historical reflections of Immanuel.

Know Immanuel.

Embrace Immanuel.

Worship Immanuel.

Immanuel, God with us.

---

1. As a parallel, see John 21:25.

CONCLUSION: REFLECTIONS OF IMMANUEL

Questions for Reflection

1. It is refreshing to realize that God has always been Immanuel, God with us—even when we least expect it. We considered many examples from Scripture. Are there others you can think of that we did not discuss?

2. Is there a recent situation in your life that allowed you to become more aware of God's Immanuel presence? Right now, where might you most need to experience God's faithful, Immanuel presence?

COLLECT: CONTEMPORARY

The Nativity of Our Lord: Christmas Day

O God, you make us glad by the yearly festival of the birth of your only Son Jesus Christ: Grant that we, who joyfully receive him as our Redeemer, may with sure confidence behold him when he comes to be our Judge; who lives and reigns with you and the Holy Spirit, one God, now and for ever. *Amen.*[1]

---

1. *BCP*, 212.

Bibliography

Brueggemann, Walter. *Celebrating Abundance: Devotions for Advent*. Louisville, KY: Westminster John Knox, 2017.

———. *The Prophetic Imagination*. 2nd ed. Minneapolis, MN: Fortress, 2001.

Calhoun, Adele Ahlberg. *Spiritual Disciplines Handbook: Practices That Transform Us*. Rev. ed. Downers Grove, IL: InterVarsity, 2015.

Castleman, Robbie F. *Story-Shaped Worship: Following Patterns from the Bible and History*. Downers Grove, IL: InterVarsity Academic, 2013.

Dodd, Chip. *The Voice of the Heart: A Call to Full Living*. 2nd ed. Nashville, TN: Sage Hill, 2014.

Episcopal Church. *The Book of Common Prayer and Administration of the Sacraments and Other Rites and Ceremonies of the Church: Together with the Psalter or Psalms of David according to the Use of the Episcopal Church*. New York: Oxford University Press, 2008.

Foster, Richard. *Celebration of Discipline: The Path to Spiritual Growth*. 3rd ed. San Francisco: HarperSanFrancisco, 1998.

France, R.T. *The Gospel of Matthew*. The New International Commentary on the New Testament. Grand Rapids, MI: Eerdmans, 2007.

Fuerst, Tom. *Underdogs and Outsiders: A Bible Study on the Untold Stories of Advent*. Nashville, TN: Abingdon, 2016.

Green, Joel B. *The Gospel of Luke*. The New International Commentary on the New Testament. Grand Rapids, MI: Eerdmans, 1997.

Ireton, K.C. *The Circle of Seasons: Meeting God in the Church Year*. 10th anniversary ed. Edmonds, WA: Mason Lewis, 2018.

Longman, Tremper, III. *How to Read the Psalms*. Downers Grove, IL: InterVarsity, 1988.

Merton, Thomas. *Seasons of Celebration: Meditations on the Cycle of Liturgical Feasts*. Notre Dame, IN: Ave Maria, 2009.

Morris, Leon. *The Gospel According to John*. Rev. ed. The New International Commentary on the New Testament. Grand Rapids, MI: Eerdmans, 1995.

Motyer, J. Alec. *The Prophecy of Isaiah: An Introduction & Commentary*. Downers Grove, IL: InterVarsity, 1993.

Nouwen, Henri J.M. *Here and Now: Living in the Spirit*. New York: Crossroad, 2013.

Peterson, Eugene H. *As Kingfishers Catch Fire: A Conversation on the Ways of God Formed by the Words of God*. New York: WaterBrook, 2017.

———. *Christ Plays in Ten Thousand Places: A Conversation in Spiritual Theology*. Grand Rapids, MI: Eerdmans, 2008.

———. *Eat This Book: A Conversation in the Art of Spiritual Reading*. Grand Rapids, MI: Eerdmans, 2006.

———. *A Long Obedience in the Same Direction: Discipleship in an Instant Society*. Downers Grove, IL: InterVarsity, 2000.

Ramsey, Russ. *The Advent of the Lamb of God*. Downers Grove, IL: InterVarsity, 2018.

Rohr, Richard. *Things Hidden: Scripture as Spirituality*. Cincinnati, OH: Franciscan Media, 2008.

Seuss, Dr. *How the Grinch Stole Christmas!*. New York: Random House, 1957.

Smith, James K.A. *Desiring the Kingdom: Worship, Worldview, and Cultural Formation*. Grand Rapids, MI: Baker Academic, 2009.

Tozer, A.W. *And He Dwelt Among Us: Teachings from the Gospel of John*. Compiled and edited by James L. Snyder. Ventura, CA: Regal, 2009.

Warren, Tish Harrison. *Liturgy of the Ordinary: Sacred Practices in Everyday Life*. Downers Grove, IL: InterVarsity, 2016.

Watts, John D.W. *Isaiah 1–33*. Vol. 24, *Word Biblical Commentary*. Nashville, TN: Thomas Nelson, 1985.

Webber, Robert E. *Ancient-Future Time: Forming Spirituality through the Christian Year*. Grand Rapids, MI: Baker, 2004.

Wright, Chris. *Knowing Jesus through the Old Testament*. Downers Grove, IL: InterVarsity Academic, 1992.

CPSIA information can be obtained
at www.ICGtesting.com
Printed in the USA
JSHW021351131020
8731JS00009B/9